Cram101 Textbook Outlines to accompany:

Probation, Parole, and Community Corrections

Champion, 4th Edition

An Academic Internet Publishers (AIPI) publication (c) 2007.

You have a discounted membership at www.Cram101.com with this book.

Get all of the practice tests for the chapters of this textbook, and access in-depth reference material for writing essays and papers. Here is an example from a Cram101 Biology text:

Multiple Choice Results:

Human Biology: Concepts and Current Issues
Johnson, 3rd Edition, Pearson Education

100%

I WANT A BETTER GRADE   The Chemistry of Living Things   Items 1 - 50 of 172.

1. _____ is a chemical compound that contains oxygen, hydrogen, and carbon atoms. They consist of monosaccharide sugars of varying chain lengths and that have the general chemical formula $C_nH_{2n}O_n$ or are derivatives of such.

    C Glycogen   C Carcinogen   Correct Answer:
    ⊙ Carbohydrate   C Protein   Carbohydrate

2. Obligate intracellular parasite of living cells consisting of an outer capsid and an inner core of nucleic acid is referred to as _____. The term _____ usually refers to those particles that infect eukaryotes whilst the term bacteriophage or phage is used to describe those infecting prokaryotes.

    C Single bond   C Virus   Correct Answer:
    C Biology   C Glucose   Virus

3. Stored energy as a result of location or spatial arrangement is referred to as _____.

    C Digestive tract   C Carcinogen   Correct Answer:
    C Vitamin   C Potential energy   Potential energy

4. _____ is a chemical element in the periodic table that has the symbol C and atomic number 6. An abundant nonmetallic, tetravalent element, _____ has several allotropic forms.

    C Solvent   C Carbon   Correct Answer:
    C Metabolism   C Tertiary structure Carbon

5. _____ is an essential amino acid. The genetic disorder phenylketonuria is an inability to metabolize _____.

    C Glycerol   C Hydrocarbon   Correct Answer:
    C Phenylalanine   C Polypeptide   Phenylalanine

When you need problem solving help with math, stats, and other disciplines, www.Cram101.com will walk through the formulas and solutions step by step.

With Cram101.com online, you also have access to extensive reference material.

You will nail those essays and papers. Here is an example from a Cram101 Biology text:

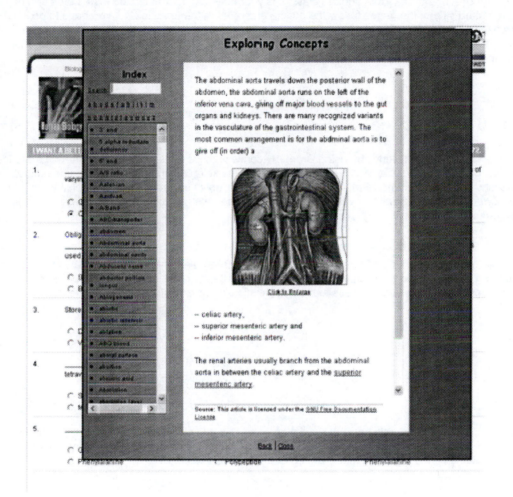

Visit **www.Cram101.com**, click Sign Up at the top of the screen, and enter DK73DW852 in the promo code box on the registration screen. Access to www.Cram101.com is normally $9.95, but because you have purchased this book, your access fee is only $4.95. Sign up and stop highlighting textbooks forever.

Learning System

Cram101 Textbook Outlines is a learning system. The notes in this book are the highlights of your textbook, you will never have to highlight a book again.

How to use this book. Take this book to class, it is your notebook for the lecture. The notes and highlights on the left hand side of the pages follow the outline and order of the textbook. All you have to do is follow along while your intructor presents the lecture. Circle the items emphasized in class and add other important information on the right side. With Cram101 Textbook Outlines you'll spend less time writing and more time listening. Learning becomes more efficient.

Cram101.com Online

Increase your studying efficiency by using Cram101.com's practice tests and online reference material. It is the perfect complement to Cram101 Textbook Outlines. Use self-teaching matching tests or simulate in-class testing with comprehensive multiple choice tests, or simply use Cram's true and false tests for quick review. Cram101.com even allows you to enter your in-class notes for an integrated studying format combining the textbook notes with your class notes.

Visit **www.Cram101.com**, click Sign Up at the top of the screen, and enter **DK73DW852** in the promo code box on the registration screen. Access to www.Cram101.com is normally $9.95, but because you have purchased this book, your access fee is only $4.95. Sign up and stop highlighting textbooks forever.

Probation, Parole, and Community Corrections
Champion, 4th

CONTENTS

Battery	In many common law jurisdictions, the crime of battery involves an injury or other contact upon the person of another in a manner likely to cause bodily harm.
Felony	The term felony is used for very serious crimes, whereas misdemeanors are considered to be less serious offenses. It is a crime punishable by one or more years of imprisonment.
Probation	Nonpunitive, legal disposition of juveniles emphasizing community treatment in which the juvenile is closely supervised by an officer of the court and must adhere to a strict set of rules to avoid incarceration is probation.
Restitution	The law of restitution is the law of gains-based recovery. When a court orders restitution it orders the defendant to give up his gains to the claimant.
Community	Community refers to a group of people who share a common sense of identity and interact with one another on a sustained basis.
Cocaine	Cocaine is a crystalline tropane alkaloid that is obtained from the leaves of the coca plant. It is a stimulant of the central nervous system and an appetite suppressant, creating what has been described as a euphoric sense of happiness and increased energy.
Crime	Crime refers to any action that violates criminal laws established by political authority. A crime in a nontechnical sense is an act that violates a very important political or moral command.
Authority	Authority refers to power that is attached to a position that others perceive as legitimate.
Violent crime	A violent crime or crime of violence is a crime in which the offender uses or threatens to use violent force upon the victim. The United States Department of Justice Bureau of Justice Statistics (BJS) counts five categories of crime as violent crimes: murder, rape, robbery, aggravated assault, and simple assault.
Criminal justice	Criminal justice refers to the system used by government to maintain social control, enforce laws, and administer justice. Law enforcement (police), courts, and corrections are the primary agencies charged with these responsibilities.
National Crime Victimization Survey	The National Crime Victimization Survey (NCVS), administered by the Bureau of Justice Statistics, is a national survey of approximately 42,000 households in the United States, on the frequency of crime victimization, as well as chacteristics and consequences of victimization.
Uniform Crime Reports	The Uniform Crime Reports are crime indexes, published annually by the Federal Bureau of Investigation (FBI). The reports summarize the incidence and rate of reported crimes within the United States.
Society	A society is a grouping of individuals, which is characterized by common interest and may have distinctive culture and institutions.
Mean	In statistics, mean has two related meanings: a)the average in ordinary English, which is also called the arithmetic mean (and is distinguished from the geometric mean or harmonic mean). The average is also called sample mean. b)the expected value of a random variable, which is also called the population mean.
Juvenile justice system	The segment of the justice system including law enforcement officers, the courts, and correctional agencies, designed to treat youthful offenders is referred to as the juvenile justice system.
Sex offender	A sex offender is a person who has been criminally charged and convicted of, or has pled guilty to, a sex crime. As a label of identity it is used in criminal psychology.
Recidivism	The probability that those incarcerated and then released are likely to return to prison for the commission of new crimes is referred to as recidivism.
Jurisdiction	Jurisdiction refers to every kind of judicial action; the authority of courts and judicial officers to decide cases.
Organization	In sociology organization is understood as planned, coordinated and purposeful action of human beings

	to construct or compile a common tangible or intangible product or service.
Aggregate	Aggregate refers to a collection of people who happen to be in the same place at the same time.
Aggravated Assault	Aggravated assault refers to an unlawful attack by one person upon another for the purpose of inflicting severe or aggravated bodily injury.
Burglary	Burglary – also called breaking and entering or house breaking – is a crime related to theft. It typically involves someone breaking into a house with an intent to commit a crime.
Robbery	The unlawful taking of, or the attempt to take something of value from another person or persons by using violence or the threat of violence, is referred to as a robbery.
Murder	Murder is the unlawful, premeditated killing of a human being by another. The penalty for murder is usually either life imprisonment, or in jurisdictions with capital punishment, the death penalty.
Rape	Rape is the act of forcing penetrative sexual acts, against another's will through violence, force, threat of injury, or other duress, or where the victim is unable to decline, due to the effects of drugs or alcohol.
Sexual abuse	Sexual abuse is defined by the forcing of undesired sexual acts by one person to another.
Embezzlement	Embezzlement is the fraudulent appropriation by a person to his own use of property or money entrusted to that person's care but owned by someone else.
Larceny	Larceny is the trespassory taking and asportation of the (tangible) personal property of another with the intent to deprive him or her of it permanently.
Statistics	Statistics is a mathematical science pertaining to the collection, analysis, interpretation, and presentation of data. It is applicable to a wide variety of academic disciplines, from the physical and social sciences to the humanities; it is also used and misused for making informed decisions in all areas of business and government.
Crime statistics	Crime statistics attempt to provide a statistical measure of the level, or amount, of crime that is prevalent in societies. Given that crime, by definition, is an illegal activity, every way of measuring it is likely to be inaccurate.
Index offenses	Whether they are committed by juveniles or adults, these criminal acts, such as robbery, rape, and homicide are referred to as index offenses.
Manslaughter	Manslaughter refers to the killing of another person through gross negligence or without specific intent.
Government	A government is a body that has the authority to make and the power to enforce laws within a civil, corporate, religious, academic, or other organization or group.
Census	A census is the process of obtaining information about every member of a population. It can be contrasted with sampling in which information is only obtained from a subset of a population. As such it is a method used for accumulating statistical data, and it is also vital to democracy.
Victimizations	Victimizations refer to the number of people who are victims of criminal acts; young teens are fifteen times more likely than older adults to be victims of crimes.
Vested interest	An expectation of private gain that often underlies the expressed interest in a public issue is a vested interest.
Personality disorder	Personality disorder refers to a mental disorder characterized by a set of inflexible, maladaptive personality traits that keep a person from functioning properly in society.
Ritual	A ritual is a set of actions, performed mainly for their symbolic value, which is prescribed by a religion or by the traditions of a community.
Range	A measure of variability defined as the high score in a distribution minus the low score is referred to

as a range.

Detention	Temporary care of a child alleged to be delinquent who requires secure custody in physically restricting facilities pending court disposition or execution of a court order is detention.
Probable cause	Reasonable ground to believe the existence of facts that an offense was committed and that the accused committed that offense is called probable cause.
Immigration	Although human migration has existed for hundreds of thousands of years, immigration in the modern sense refers to movement of people from one nation-state to another, where they are not citizens.
Subculture	A group within the broader society that has values, norms and lifestyle distinct from those of the majority, is referred to as a subculture.
Plea bargain	A plea bargain is an agreement in a criminal case in which a prosecutor and a defendant arrange to settle the case against the defendant. The defendant agrees to plead guilty or no contest (and often allocute) in exchange for some agreement from the prosecutor as to the punishment.
Grand jury	A grand jury is a type of jury, in the common law legal system, which determines if there is enough evidence for a trial.
Punishment	Punishment is the practice of imposing something unpleasant on a subject as a response to some unwanted behavior or disobedience that the subject has displayed.
Community service	Community service refers to service that a person performs for the benefit of his or her local community. People become involved in community service for a range of reasons, for some, it is an altruistic act, for others it is a punishment.
Deterrence	Deterrence is a theory from behavioral psychology about preventing or controlling actions or behavior through fear of punishment or retribution. This theory of criminology is shaping the criminal justice system of the United States and various other countries.

Probation	Nonpunitive, legal disposition of juveniles emphasizing community treatment in which the juvenile is closely supervised by an officer of the court and must adhere to a strict set of rules to avoid incarceration is probation.
Community	Community refers to a group of people who share a common sense of identity and interact with one another on a sustained basis.
Electronic monitoring	Electronic monitoring refers to active monitoring systems consist of a radio transmitter worn by the offender that sends a continuous signal to the probation department computer, alerting officials if the offender leaves his or her place of confinement; passive systems employ computer-generated random phone calls that must be responded to in a certain period of time from a particular phone or other device.
House arrest	House arrest refers to an offender is required to stay at home during specific periods of time; monitoring is done by random phone calls and visits or by electronic devices.
Felony	The term felony is used for very serious crimes, whereas misdemeanors are considered to be less serious offenses. It is a crime punishable by one or more years of imprisonment.
Juvenile court	Court that has original jurisdiction over persons defined by statute as juveniles and alleged to be delinquents, status offenders, or dependents is called juvenile court.
Detention	Temporary care of a child alleged to be delinquent who requires secure custody in physically restricting facilities pending court disposition or execution of a court order is detention.
Government	A government is a body that has the authority to make and the power to enforce laws within a civil, corporate, religious, academic, or other organization or group.
Jurisdiction	Jurisdiction refers to every kind of judicial action; the authority of courts and judicial officers to decide cases.
Punishment	Punishment is the practice of imposing something unpleasant on a subject as a response to some unwanted behavior or disobedience that the subject has displayed.
Sanction	A punishment for nonconformity that reinforces socially approved forms of behavior is a sanction.
Community service	Community service refers to service that a person performs for the benefit of his or her local community. People become involved in community service for a range of reasons, for some, it is an altruistic act, for others it is a punishment.
Restitution	The law of restitution is the law of gains-based recovery. When a court orders restitution it orders the defendant to give up his gains to the claimant.
Public opinion	Public opinion is the aggregate of individual attitudes or beliefs held by the adult population.
Group therapy	Group therapy is a form of psychotherapy during which one or several therapists treat a small group of clients together as a group. This may be more cost effective than individual therapy, and possibly even more productive.
Organization	In sociology organization is understood as planned, coordinated and purposeful action of human beings to construct or compile a common tangible or intangible product or service.
Criminal justice	Criminal justice refers to the system used by government to maintain social control, enforce laws, and administer justice. Law enforcement (police), courts, and corrections are the primary agencies charged with these responsibilities.
Mean	In statistics, mean has two related meanings: a)the average in ordinary English, which is also called the arithmetic mean (and is distinguished from the geometric mean or harmonic mean). The average is also called sample mean. b)the expected value of a random variable,

	which is also called the population mean.
Crime	Crime refers to any action that violates criminal laws established by political authority. A crime in a nontechnical sense is an act that violates a very important political or moral command.
Society	A society is a grouping of individuals, which is characterized by common interest and may have distinctive culture and institutions.
Neighborhood	A neighborhood is a geographically localized community located within a larger city, town or suburb. Traditionally, a neighborhood is small enough that the neighbors are all able to know each other.
Coping	Efforts to control, reduce, or learn to tolerate the threats that lead to stress is referred to as coping.
Recidivism	The probability that those incarcerated and then released are likely to return to prison for the commission of new crimes is referred to as recidivism.
Range	A measure of variability defined as the high score in a distribution minus the low score is referred to as a range.
Disability	A physical or health condition that stigmatizes or causes discrimination, is referred to as a disability.
Addiction	A pattern of behavior characterized by an overwhelming involvement with using a drug and securing its supply is defined as an addiction.
Sector	Sector refers to parts of the economy as judged by the economic activity that they constitute. For example agriculture, forestry, fishing and mining constitute the primary sector.
Compliance	Conforming behavior that occurs in response to direct social pressure is referred to as compliance.
Substance abuse	Substance abuse refers to the overindulgence in and dependence on a psychoactive leading to effects that are detrimental to the individual's physical health or mental health, or the welfare of others.
Control group	A group of people in an experiment who are not exposed to the experimental stimulus under study are referred to as a control group.
Statistics	Statistics is a mathematical science pertaining to the collection, analysis, interpretation, and presentation of data. It is applicable to a wide variety of academic disciplines, from the physical and social sciences to the humanities; it is also used and misused for making informed decisions in all areas of business and government.
Crime rate	Crime rate is a measure of the rate of occurrence of crimes committed in a given area and time. Most commonly, crime rate is given as the number of crimes committed among a given number of persons.
Group home	A Group home is a structure designed or converted to serve as a non-secure home for persons who share a common characteristic. In the United States, the term most often refers to homes designed for those in need of social assistance, and who are usually deemed incapable of living alone or without proper supervision.
Attitude	Attitude refers to an enduring mental representation of a person, place, or thing that evokes an emotional response and related behavior.
Fear of crime	The fear of crime refers to the fear of being a victim of crime. Usually the fear is disproportionate to the likihood of being a victim of crime. Moral panics are often the cause

	of the rizing fear of crime.
Mills	Mills is best remembered for studying the structure of Power in the U.S. in his book, The Power Elite. Mills was concerned with the responsibilities of intellectuals in post-World War II society, and advocated relevance and engagement over disinterested academic observation, as a "public intelligence apparatus" in challenging the crackpot policies of these institutional elite in the "Big Three", the economic, political and military.
Empathy	Empathy is commonly defined as one's ability to recognize, perceive and directly experientially feel the emotion of another. As the states of mind, beliefs, and desires of others are intertwined with their emotions, one with empathy for another may often be able to more effectively divine another's modes of thought and mood.
Vested interest	An expectation of private gain that often underlies the expressed interest in a public issue is a vested interest.
Public sector	Public sector refers to that part of a national economy subject to direct government ownership and control. The constituents of the public sector are the departments of central and local government, various government agencies and the nationalized industries.
Motive	Motive refers to a hypothetical state within an organism that propels the organism toward a goal. In criminal law a motive is the cause that moves people and induce a certain action.
Sex offender	A sex offender is a person who has been criminally charged and convicted of, or has pled guilty to, a sex crime. As a label of identity it is used in criminal psychology.
Shoplifting	Shoplifting (also known as retail theft) is theft of merchandise for sale in a shop, store, or other retail establishment, by an ostensible patron. It is one of the most common crimes for police and courts.
Burglary	Burglary – also called breaking and entering or house breaking – is a crime related to theft. It typically involves someone breaking into a house with an intent to commit a crime.
Violent crime	A violent crime or crime of violence is a crime in which the offender uses or threatens to use violent force upon the victim. The United States Department of Justice Bureau of Justice Statistics (BJS) counts five categories of crime as violent crimes: murder, rape, robbery, aggravated assault, and simple assault.
Social control	A social mechanism that regulates individual and group behavior through sanctions and rewards is a social control.
Bias	A bias is a prejudice in a general or specific sense, usually in the sense for having a preference to one particular point of view or ideological perspective.
Technology	The application of logic, reason and knowledge to the problems of exploiting raw materials from the environment, is referred to as a technology.
Battery	In many common law jurisdictions, the crime of battery involves an injury or other contact upon the person of another in a manner likely to cause bodily harm.
Depression	In the field of psychiatry, the word depression can also have this meaning of low mood but more specifically refers to a mental illness when it has reached a severity and duration to warrant a diagnosis, whether there is an obvious situational cause or not.
Discrimination	Discrimination refers to the denial of equal access to social resources to people on the basis of their group membership.
Deterrence	Deterrence is a theory from behavioral psychology about preventing or controlling actions or behavior through fear of punishment or retribution. This theory of criminology is shaping the criminal justice system of the United States and various other countries.

Authority	Authority refers to power that is attached to a position that others perceive as legitimate.
Narcotic	A narcotic is an addictive drug, derived from opium, that reduces pain, induces sleep and may alter mood or behavior.
Professional-zation	The social process through which an occupation acquires the cultural and structural characteristics of a profession is professionalization.

Go to **Cram101.com** for the Practice Tests for this Chapter.

Neighborhood	A neighborhood is a geographically localized community located within a larger city, town or suburb. Traditionally, a neighborhood is small enough that the neighbors are all able to know each other.
Burglary	Burglary – also called breaking and entering or house breaking – is a crime related to theft. It typically involves someone breaking into a house with an intent to commit a crime.
Crime	Crime refers to any action that violates criminal laws established by political authority. A crime in a nontechnical sense is an act that violates a very important political or moral command.
Extortion	Extortion is a criminal offense, which occurs when a person either obtains money or property from another through coercion or intimidation or threatens one with physical harm unless they are paid money or property.
Government	A government is a body that has the authority to make and the power to enforce laws within a civil, corporate, religious, academic, or other organization or group.
Murder	Murder is the unlawful, premeditated killing of a human being by another. The penalty for murder is usually either life imprisonment, or in jurisdictions with capital punishment, the death penalty.
Aggravated Assault	Aggravated assault refers to an unlawful attack by one person upon another for the purpose of inflicting severe or aggravated bodily injury.
Mean	In statistics, mean has two related meanings: a)the average in ordinary English, which is also called the arithmetic mean (and is distinguished from the geometric mean or harmonic mean). The average is also called sample mean. b)the expected value of a random variable, which is also called the population mean.
Punishment	Punishment is the practice of imposing something unpleasant on a subject as a response to some unwanted behavior or disobedience that the subject has displayed.
Socioeconomic status	An overall rank based on characteristics such as education and occupation, used to describe people's positions in stratification systems is referred to as socioeconomic status.
Gender	Gender refers to socially defined behavior regarded as appropriate for the members of each
Probation	Nonpunitive, legal disposition of juveniles emphasizing community treatment in which the juvenile is closely supervised by an officer of the court and must adhere to a strict set of rules to avoid incarceration is probation.
Felony	The term felony is used for very serious crimes, whereas misdemeanors are considered to be less serious offenses. It is a crime punishable by one or more years of imprisonment.
Victim impact statement	A victim impact statement is a written or verbal statement made as part of the judicial legal process, which allows a victim of crime the opportunity to speak during the sentencing of their attacker or at subsequent parole hearings.
Jurisdiction	Jurisdiction refers to every kind of judicial action; the authority of courts and judicial officers to decide cases.
Deterrence	Deterrence is a theory from behavioral psychology about preventing or controlling actions or behavior through fear of punishment or retribution. This theory of criminology is shaping the criminal justice system of the United States and various other countries.
Community	Community refers to a group of people who share a common sense of identity and interact with one another on a sustained basis.
Violent crime	A violent crime or crime of violence is a crime in which the offender uses or threatens to use violent force upon the victim. The United States Department of Justice Bureau of Justice

	Statistics (BJS) counts five categories of crime as violent crimes: murder, rape, robbery, aggravated assault, and simple assault.
Sanction	A punishment for nonconformity that reinforces socially approved forms of behavior is a sanction.
Abandonment	Parents that physically leave their children with the intention of completely severing the parent-child relationship are engaging in abandonment. To give up control of a child, legally terminating parental rights; in many states abandonment is considered child abuse.
Robbery	The unlawful taking of, or the attempt to take something of value from another person or persons by using violence or the threat of violence, is referred to as a robbery.
Life expectancy	The number of years a newborn in a particular society can expect to live is referred to as a life expectancy.
Range	A measure of variability defined as the high score in a distribution minus the low score is referred to as a range.
Mandatory sentence	A criminal sentence that is defined by a statutory requirement that states the penalty to be set for all cases of a specific offense is called a mandatory sentence.
Community service	Community service refers to service that a person performs for the benefit of his or her local community. People become involved in community service for a range of reasons, for some, it is an altruistic act, for others it is a punishment.
Restitution	The law of restitution is the law of gains-based recovery. When a court orders restitution it orders the defendant to give up his gains to the claimant.
Criminal justice	Criminal justice refers to the system used by government to maintain social control, enforce laws, and administer justice. Law enforcement (police), courts, and corrections are the primary agencies charged with these responsibilities.
Marital status	A person's marital status describes their relationship with a significant other. Some common statuses are: married, single, separated, divorced, widowed, engaged, invalid, annulled, living common-law. The number of children may also be specified and, in this case, becomes synonymous with family status. For example: married with no children. Marital status is often a question on censuses, credit card applications, and many different polls.
Addiction	A pattern of behavior characterized by an overwhelming involvement with using a drug and securing its supply is defined as an addiction.
Statistics	Statistics is a mathematical science pertaining to the collection, analysis, interpretation, and presentation of data. It is applicable to a wide variety of academic disciplines, from the physical and social sciences to the humanities; it is also used and misused for making informed decisions in all areas of business and government.
Society	A society is a grouping of individuals, which is characterized by common interest and may have distinctive culture and institutions.
Intake	Intake refers to process during which a juvenile referral is received and a decision is made to file a petition in juvenile court to release the juvenile, to place the juvenile under supervision, or to refer the juvenile elsewhere.
Sexual abuse	Sexual abuse is defined by the forcing of undesired sexual acts by one person to another.
Detention	Temporary care of a child alleged to be delinquent who requires secure custody in physically restricting facilities pending court disposition or execution of a court order is detention.
Adaptation	Adaptation refers to the ability of a sociocultural system to change with the demands of a changing physical or social environment.

Frequency	In statistics the frequency of an event i is the number n_i of times the event occurred in the experiment or the study.
Authority	Authority refers to power that is attached to a position that others perceive as legitimate.
Wilson	In The Declining Significance of Race: Blacks and Changing American Institutions Wilson argues that the significance of race is waning, and an African-American's class is comparatively more important in determining his or her life chances.
Public defender	In the United States, a public defender is a lawyer whose duty is to provide legal counsel and representation to indigent defendants in criminal cases who are unable to pay for legal assistance.
Cocaine	Cocaine is a crystalline tropane alkaloid that is obtained from the leaves of the coca plant. It is a stimulant of the central nervous system and an appetite suppressant, creating what has been described as a euphoric sense of happiness and increased energy.
Larceny	Larceny is the trespassory taking and asportation of the (tangible) personal property of another with the intent to deprive him or her of it permanently.
Alcoholism	Alcoholism refers to a disorder that involves long-term, repeated, uncontrolled, compulsive, and excessive use of alcoholic beverages and that impairs the drinker's health, work and social relationships.
Sexual assault	Sexual assault is any undesired physical contact of a sexual nature perpetrated against another person. While associated with rape, sexual assault is much broader and the specifics may vary according to social, political or legal definition.
Immigration	Although human migration has existed for hundreds of thousands of years, immigration in the modern sense refers to movement of people from one nation-state to another, where they are not citizens.
Cannabis	The hemp plant from which marijuana, hashish, and THC are derived is referred to as cannabis.
Social history	Social history is an area of historical study considered by some to be a social science that attempts to view historical evidence from the point of view of developing social trends. In this view, it may include areas of economic history, legal history and the analysis of other aspects of civil society that show the evolution of social norms, behaviors and more.
Mental hospital	A medical institution specializing in providing inpatient care for psychological disorders is a psychiatric hospital or mental hospital.
Rape	Rape is the act of forcing penetrative sexual acts, against another's will through violence, force, threat of injury, or other duress, or where the victim is unable to decline, due to the effects of drugs or alcohol.
Taylor	Taylor was an American engineer who sought to improve industrial efficiency. He was one of the intellectual leaders of the Efficiency Movement and his ideas, broadly conceived, were highly influential in the Progressive Era. During the latter part of his career he was a management consultant, and he is sometimes called "The Father of Scientific Management."
Grand jury	A grand jury is a type of jury, in the common law legal system, which determines if there is enough evidence for a trial.
Drug dependence	The condition, which may or may not stem from physiological withdrawal symptoms, in which a person feels compelled to take a particular drug on a regular basis, is referred to as drug dependence.
Compliance	Conforming behavior that occurs in response to direct social pressure is referred to as compliance.

General deterrence	General deterrence refers to crime control policies that depend on the fear of criminal penalties, such as long prison sentences for violent crimes; aim is to convince law violator that the pain outweighs the benefit of criminal activity.
Embezzlement	Embezzlement is the fraudulent appropriation by a person to his own use of property or money entrusted to that person's care but owned by someone else.

22

Go to **Cram101.com** for the Practice Tests for this Chapter.

Robbery	The unlawful taking of, or the attempt to take something of value from another person or persons by using violence or the threat of violence, is referred to as a robbery.
Mental hospital	A medical institution specializing in providing inpatient care for psychological disorders is a psychiatric hospital or mental hospital.
Insanity	Insanity refers to a legal status indicating that a person cannot be held responsible for his or her actions because of mental illness.
Murder	Murder is the unlawful, premeditated killing of a human being by another. The penalty for murder is usually either life imprisonment, or in jurisdictions with capital punishment, the death penalty.
Government	A government is a body that has the authority to make and the power to enforce laws within a civil, corporate, religious, academic, or other organization or group.
Probation	Nonpunitive, legal disposition of juveniles emphasizing community treatment in which the juvenile is closely supervized by an officer of the court and must adhere to a strict set of rules to avoid incarceration is probation.
Rape	Rape is the act of forcing penetrative sexual acts, against another's will through violence, force, threat of injury, or other duress, or where the victim is unable to decline, due to the effects of drugs or alcohol.
Community service	Community service refers to service that a person performs for the benefit of his or her local community. People become involved in community service for a range of reasons, for some, it is an altruistic act, for others it is a punishment.
Community	Community refers to a group of people who share a common sense of identity and interact with one another on a sustained basis.
Stigmatized	People who have been negatively labeled because of their participation, or alleged participation, in deviant or outlawed behaviors are referred to as stigmatized.
Restorative justice	Restorative justice is commonly known as a theory of criminal justice that focuses on crime as an act against another individual or community rather than the state. The victim plays a major role in the process and may receive some type of restitution from the offender.
Crime	Crime refers to any action that violates criminal laws established by political authority. A crime in a nontechnical sense is an act that violates a very important political or moral command.
Sanction	A punishment for nonconformity that reinforces socially approved forms of behavior is a sanction.
Criminal law	Criminal law (also known as penal law) is the body of statutory and common law that deals with crime and the legal punishment of criminal offenses. There are four theories of criminal justice: punishment, deterrence, incapacitation, and rehabilitation.
Punishment	Punishment is the practice of imposing something unpleasant on a subject as a response to some unwanted behavior or disobedience that the subject has displayed.
Separation of powers	American structural concept of government in which power is horizontally and vertically divided so that no one unit of government becomes too powerful is referred to as separation of powers.
Motive	Motive refers to a hypothetical state within an organism that propels the organism toward a goal. In criminal law a motive is the cause that moves people and induce a certain action.
Authority	Authority refers to power that is attached to a position that others perceive as legitimate.
Mean	In statistics, mean has two related meanings: a)the average in ordinary English, which is

24

	also called the arithmetic mean (and is distinguished from the geometric mean or harmonic mean). The average is also called sample mean. b)the expected value of a random variable, which is also called the population mean.
Embezzlement	Embezzlement is the fraudulent appropriation by a person to his own use of property or money entrusted to that person's care but owned by someone else.
Felony	The term felony is used for very serious crimes, whereas misdemeanors are considered to be less serious offenses. It is a crime punishable by one or more years of imprisonment.
Society	A society is a grouping of individuals, which is characterized by common interest and may have distinctive culture and institutions.
Juvenile delinquency	Juvenile delinquency refers to antisocial or criminal acts performed by minors. It is an important social issue because juveniles are capable of committing serious crimes, but most legal systems prescribe specific procedures and punishments for dealing with such crimes.
Juvenile court	Court that has original jurisdiction over persons defined by statute as juveniles and alleged to be delinquents, status offenders, or dependents is called juvenile court.
Brockway	Brockway was a penologist and is sometimes regarded as the "Father of prison reform" in the United States of America.
Electronic monitoring	Electronic monitoring refers to active monitoring systems consist of a radio transmitter worn by the offender that sends a continuous signal to the probation department computer, alerting officials if the offender leaves his or her place of confinement; passive systems employ computer-generated random phone calls that must be responded to in a certain period of time from a particular phone or other device.
Jurisdiction	Jurisdiction refers to every kind of judicial action; the authority of courts and judicial officers to decide cases.
Medical model	The application of the medical perspective in explaining and treating troublesome human behavior, is referred to as a medical model.
Gender	Gender refers to socially defined behavior regarded as appropriate for the members of each
Encounter group	Encounter group refers to a type of group that fosters self-awareness by focusing on how group members relate to one another in a setting that encourages open expression of feelings.
Group therapy	Group therapy is a form of psychotherapy during which one or several therapists treat a small group of clients together as a group. This may be more cost effective than individual therapy, and possibly even more productive.
Prison riot	A prison riot is a riot that occurs in a prison, usually when those incarcerated rebel openly against correctional officials. It is usually instigated by prisoners who claim that the administration are degrading them, either by direct physical, or psychological force.
Socioeconomic status	An overall rank based on characteristics such as education and occupation, used to describe people's positions in stratification systems is referred to as socioeconomic status.
Progressive Era	In the United States, the Progressive Era was a period of reform which lasted from the 1890s through the 1920s. The reformers advocated the Efficiency Movement. Progressives assumed that anything old was encrusted with inefficient and useless practices. A scientific study of the problem would enable experts to discover the "one best solution."
Recidivism	The probability that those incarcerated and then released are likely to return to prison for the commission of new crimes is referred to as recidivism.
Crime rate	Crime rate is a measure of the rate of occurrence of crimes committed in a given area and time. Most commonly, crime rate is given as the number of crimes committed among a given

number of persons.

Due process	Basic constitutional principle based on the concept of the primacy of the individual and the complementary concept of limitation on governmental power; safeguards the individual from unfair state procedures in judicial or administrative proceedings; due process rights have been extended to juvenile trials.
Range	A measure of variability defined as the high score in a distribution minus the low score is referred to as a range.
Restitution	The law of restitution is the law of gains-based recovery. When a court orders restitution it orders the defendant to give up his gains to the claimant.
Burglary	Burglary – also called breaking and entering or house breaking – is a crime related to theft. It typically involves someone breaking into a house with an intent to commit a crime.
Adaptation	Adaptation refers to the ability of a sociocultural system to change with the demands of a changing physical or social environment.
Coping	Efforts to control, reduce, or learn to tolerate the threats that lead to stress is referred to as coping.
Spousal abuse	Spousal abuse is a specific form of domestic violence where physical or sexual abuse is perpetuated by one spouse upon another.
Deterrence	Deterrence is a theory from behavioral psychology about preventing or controlling actions or behavior through fear of punishment or retribution. This theory of criminology is shaping the criminal justice system of the United States and various other countries.
Glaser	Glaser, American sociologist and one of the founders of the grounded theory methodology. In 1999 Glaser founded the non-profit web based organization Grounded Theory Institute.
Automation	The replacement of many workers by machines, as well as the monitoring and coordination of workers by machines with only minimal supervision from human being is referred to as automation.
Sex offender	A sex offender is a person who has been criminally charged and convicted of, or has pled guilty to, a sex crime. As a label of identity it is used in criminal psychology.
Civil rights	Civil rights are the protections and privileges of personal liberty given to all citizens by law. Civil rights are rights that are bestowed by nations on those within their territorial boundaries.
Attitude	Attitude refers to an enduring mental representation of a person, place, or thing that evokes an emotional response and related behavior.
Criminal justice	Criminal justice refers to the system used by government to maintain social control, enforce laws, and administer justice. Law enforcement (police), courts, and corrections are the primary agencies charged with these responsibilities.
Aggravated Assault	Aggravated assault refers to an unlawful attack by one person upon another for the purpose of inflicting severe or aggravated bodily injury.
Fingerprint	A fingerprint is an impression of the friction ridges of all or any part of the finger. They may be deposited in natural secretions from the eccrine glands present in friction ridge skin or they may be made by ink or other contaminants transferred from the peaks of friction skin ridges to a relatively smooth surface such as a fingerprint card.
Shoplifting	Shoplifting (also known as retail theft) is theft of merchandise for sale in a shop, store, or other retail establishment, by an ostensible patron. It is one of the most common crimes for police and courts.

Domestic violence	Domestic violence occurs when a family member, partner or ex-partner attempts to physically or psychologically dominate or harm the other.
Child abuse	Child abuse refers to not only physical assaults on a child but also malnourishment, abandonment, neglect, emotional abuse and sexual abuse.
General deterrence	General deterrence refers to crime control policies that depend on the fear of criminal penalties, such as long prison sentences for violent crimes; aim is to convince law violator that the pain outweighs the benefit of criminal activity.
Interest group	Interest group refers to an organization that attempts to affect political decisions by supporting candidates sympathetic to their interests and by influencing those already in positions of authority.
Organization	In sociology organization is understood as planned, coordinated and purposeful action of human beings to construct or compile a common tangible or intangible product or service.
Care Perspective	Care perspective refers to the moral perspective of Carol Gilligan, that views people in terms of their connectedness with others and emphasizes interpersonal communication, relationships with others and concern for others.
Interdependence	Interdependence is a dynamic of being mutually responsible to and sharing a common set of principles with others. This concept differs distinctly from "dependence" in that an interdependent relationship implies that all participants are emotionally, economically, and/or morally "independent."
Penology	Penology comprises penitentiary science: that concerned with the processes devized and adopted for the punishment, repression, and prevention of crime, and the treatment of prisoners.

American Civil Liberties Union	Lawsuits brought by the American Civil Liberties Union have been influential in the evolution of U.S. constitutional law. They provides legal assistance in cases in which it considers civil liberties to be at risk. Even when the they do not provide direct legal representation, it often submits amicus curiae briefs.
Wilson	In The Declining Significance of Race: Blacks and Changing American Institutions Wilson argues that the significance of race is waning, and an African-American's class is comparatively more important in determining his or her life chances.
Rape	Rape is the act of forcing penetrative sexual acts, against another's will through violence, force, threat of injury, or other duress, or where the victim is unable to decline, due to the effects of drugs or alcohol.
Crime	Crime refers to any action that violates criminal laws established by political authority. A crime in a nontechnical sense is an act that violates a very important political or moral command.
Probation	Nonpunitive, legal disposition of juveniles emphasizing community treatment in which the juvenile is closely supervized by an officer of the court and must adhere to a strict set of rules to avoid incarceration is probation.
Community service	Community service refers to service that a person performs for the benefit of his or her local community. People become involved in community service for a range of reasons, for some, it is an altruistic act, for others it is a punishment.
Community	Community refers to a group of people who share a common sense of identity and interact with one another on a sustained basis.
Manslaughter	Manslaughter refers to the killing of another person through gross negligence or without specific intent.
Mental hospital	A medical institution specializing in providing inpatient care for psychological disorders is a psychiatric hospital or mental hospital.
Jurisdiction	Jurisdiction refers to every kind of judicial action; the authority of courts and judicial officers to decide cases.
Compliance	Conforming behavior that occurs in response to direct social pressure is referred to as compliance.
Recidivism	The probability that those incarcerated and then released are likely to return to prison for the commission of new crimes is referred to as recidivism.
Affirmative action	Government programs intended to assure minorities and women equal hiring or admission opportunities is referred to as affirmative action.
Government	A government is a body that has the authority to make and the power to enforce laws within a civil, corporate, religious, academic, or other organization or group.
Restitution	The law of restitution is the law of gains-based recovery. When a court orders restitution it orders the defendant to give up his gains to the claimant.
Substance abuse	Substance abuse refers to the overindulgence in and dependence on a psychoactive leading to effects that are detrimental to the individual's physical health or mental health, or the welfare of others.
Narcotic	A narcotic is an addictive drug, derived from opium, that reduces pain, induces sleep and may alter mood or behavior.
Felony	The term felony is used for very serious crimes, whereas misdemeanors are considered to be less serious offenses. It is a crime punishable by one or more years of imprisonment.

Detention	Temporary care of a child alleged to be delinquent who requires secure custody in physically restricting facilities pending court disposition or execution of a court order is detention.
Organization	In sociology organization is understood as planned, coordinated and purposeful action of human beings to construct or compile a common tangible or intangible product or service.
Electronic monitoring	Electronic monitoring refers to active monitoring systems consist of a radio transmitter worn by the offender that sends a continuous signal to the probation department computer, alerting officials if the offender leaves his or her place of confinement; passive systems employ computer-generated random phone calls that must be responded to in a certain period of time from a particular phone or other device.
Mean	In statistics, mean has two related meanings: a)the average in ordinary English, which is also called the arithmetic mean (and is distinguished from the geometric mean or harmonic mean). The average is also called sample mean. b)the expected value of a random variable, which is also called the population mean.
Cocaine	Cocaine is a crystalline tropane alkaloid that is obtained from the leaves of the coca plant. It is a stimulant of the central nervous system and an appetite suppressant, creating what has been described as a euphoric sense of happiness and increased energy.
Punishment	Punishment is the practice of imposing something unpleasant on a subject as a response to some unwanted behavior or disobedience that the subject has displayed.
Range	A measure of variability defined as the high score in a distribution minus the low score is referred to as a range.
Violent crime	A violent crime or crime of violence is a crime in which the offender uses or threatens to use violent force upon the victim. The United States Department of Justice Bureau of Justice Statistics (BJS) counts five categories of crime as violent crimes: murder, rape, robbery, aggravated assault, and simple assault.
Sector	Sector refers to parts of the economy as judged by the economic activity that they constitute. For example agriculture, forestry, fishing and mining constitute the primary sector.
Aggregate	Aggregate refers to a collection of people who happen to be in the same place at the same time.
Mills	Mills is best remembered for studying the structure of Power in the U.S. in his book, The Power Elite. Mills was concerned with the responsibilities of intellectuals in post-World War II society, and advocated relevance and engagement over disinterested academic observation, as a "public intelligence apparatus" in challenging the crackpot policies of these institutional elite in the "Big Three", the economic, political and military.
Frequency	In statistics the frequency of an event i is the number n_i of times the event occurred in the experiment or the study.
Bias	A bias is a prejudice in a general or specific sense, usually in the sense for having a preference to one particular point of view or ideological perspective.
Deterrence	Deterrence is a theory from behavioral psychology about preventing or controlling actions or behavior through fear of punishment or retribution. This theory of criminology is shaping the criminal justice system of the United States and various other countries.
Authority	Authority refers to power that is attached to a position that others perceive as legitimate.
Sanction	A punishment for nonconformity that reinforces socially approved forms of behavior is a sanction.
Criminal justice	Criminal justice refers to the system used by government to maintain social control, enforce

	laws, and administer justice. Law enforcement (police), courts, and corrections are the primary agencies charged with these responsibilities.
Social skills training	Social skills training refers to a behavior therapy designed to improve interpersonal skills that emphasizes shaping, modeling, and behavioral rehearsal.
Social skill	A social skill is a skill used to interact and communicate with others to assist status in the social structure and other motivations. Social rules and social relations are created, communicated, and changed in verbal and nonverbal ways creating social complexity useful in identifying outsiders and intelligent breeding partners.
Social environment	The social environment is the direct influence of a group of individuals and their contributions to this environment, as both groups and individuals who are in frequent communication with each other within their cultural or socio-economical strata, which create role identity(-ies) and guide the individual's self (sociology) growth and their progression towards maturity.
Resocialization	Resocialization is a sociological concept dealing with the process of mentally and emotionally "re-training" a person so that he or she can operate in an environment other than that which he or she is accustomed to.
Taylor	Taylor was an American engineer who sought to improve industrial efficiency. He was one of the intellectual leaders of the Efficiency Movement and his ideas, broadly conceived, were highly influential in the Progressive Era. During the latter part of his career he was a management consultant, and he is sometimes called "The Father of Scientific Management."
Coping	Efforts to control, reduce, or learn to tolerate the threats that lead to stress is referred to as coping.
Society	A society is a grouping of individuals, which is characterized by common interest and may have distinctive culture and institutions.
Attitude	Attitude refers to an enduring mental representation of a person, place, or thing that evokes an emotional response and related behavior.
Civil rights	Civil rights are the protections and privileges of personal liberty given to all citizens by law. Civil rights are rights that are bestowed by nations on those within their territorial boundaries.
Child abuse	Child abuse refers to not only physical assaults on a child but also malnourishment, abandonment, neglect, emotional abuse and sexual abuse.
Murder	Murder is the unlawful, premeditated killing of a human being by another. The penalty for murder is usually either life imprisonment, or in jurisdictions with capital punishment, the death penalty.
Larceny	Larceny is the trespassory taking and asportation of the (tangible) personal property of another with the intent to deprive him or her of it permanently.
Gender	Gender refers to socially defined behavior regarded as appropriate for the members of each
Social role	A social role is a set of connected behaviors, rights and obligations as conceptualized by actors in a social situation. It is mostly defined as an expected behavior in a given individual social status and social position.
Criminalization	Criminalization refers to the process whereby criminal law is selectively applied to social behavior. It involves the enactment of legislation that outlaws certain types of behavior and provides for surveillance and policing of that behavior and whether or not the behavior is detected.
Crime prevention	Crime prevention is a term describing techniques used in reducing victimization as well as

deterring crime and criminals. It is applied specifically to efforts made by governments to reduce crime and law enforcement and criminal justice.

Bonding
In the social sciences, the concept of bonding refers to the formation of interpersonal relationships. Development of emotional attachment between the mother and newborn immediately after birth is considered bonding.

Mandatory sentence
A criminal sentence that is defined by a statutory requirement that states the penalty to be set for all cases of a specific offense is called a mandatory sentence.

Burglary
Burglary – also called breaking and entering or house breaking – is a crime related to theft. It typically involves someone breaking into a house with an intent to commit a crime.

Due process
Basic constitutional principle based on the concept of the primacy of the individual and the complementary concept of limitation on governmental power; safeguards the individual from unfair state procedures in judicial or administrative proceedings; due process rights have been extended to juvenile trials.

Robbery
The unlawful taking of, or the attempt to take something of value from another person or persons by using violence or the threat of violence, is referred to as a robbery.

Immunity
Immunity confers a status on a person or body that places him/her/it above the law and makes that person or body free from otherwise legal obligations such as, for example, liability for torts or damages or prosecution under criminal law for criminal acts.

Search and seizure
U.S. Constitution protects citizens from any search and seizure by police without a lawfully obtained search warrant; such warrants are issued when there is probable cause to believe that an offense has been committed.

Informant
Someone well versed in the social phenomenon that you wish to study and who is willing to tell you what he or she knows about it is an informant.

Probable cause
Reasonable ground to believe the existence of facts that an offense was committed and that the accused committed that offense is called probable cause.

Motive
Motive refers to a hypothetical state within an organism that propels the organism toward a goal. In criminal law a motive is the cause that moves people and induce a certain action.

Mail fraud
Mail fraud refers to any scheme which attempts to unlawfully obtain money or valuables in which the postal system is used at any point in the commission of a criminal offense.

Plea bargain
A plea bargain is an agreement in a criminal case in which a prosecutor and a defendant arrange to settle the case against the defendant. The defendant agrees to plead guilty or no contest (and often allocute) in exchange for some agreement from the prosecutor as to the punishment.

Addiction
A pattern of behavior characterized by an overwhelming involvement with using a drug and securing its supply is defined as an addiction.

Variable
A characteristic that varies in value or magnitude along which an object, individual or group may be categorized, such as income or age, is referred to as a variable.

Organized crime
Organized crime is crime carried out systematically by formal criminal organizations.

Gang
A gang is a group of individuals who share a common identity and, in current usage, engage in illegal activities. Historically the term referred to both criminal groups and ordinary groups of friends.

Tucker
Tucker was the leading proponent of American individualist anarchism in the 19th century. He defined 'socialism' in a very individualist manner contrary to collectivist socialists, since he supported individual ownership of property.

Criminal justice	Criminal justice refers to the system used by government to maintain social control, enforce laws, and administer justice. Law enforcement (police), courts, and corrections are the primary agencies charged with these responsibilities.
Felony	The term felony is used for very serious crimes, whereas misdemeanors are considered to be less serious offenses. It is a crime punishable by one or more years of imprisonment.
Government	A government is a body that has the authority to make and the power to enforce laws within a civil, corporate, religious, academic, or other organization or group.
Mean	In statistics, mean has two related meanings: a)the average in ordinary English, which is also called the arithmetic mean (and is distinguished from the geometric mean or harmonic mean). The average is also called sample mean. b)the expected value of a random variable, which is also called the population mean.
Probation	Nonpunitive, legal disposition of juveniles emphasizing community treatment in which the juvenile is closely supervized by an officer of the court and must adhere to a strict set of rules to avoid incarceration is probation.
Jurisdiction	Jurisdiction refers to every kind of judicial action; the authority of courts and judicial officers to decide cases.
Society	A society is a grouping of individuals, which is characterized by common interest and may have distinctive culture and institutions.
Punishment	Punishment is the practice of imposing something unpleasant on a subject as a response to some unwanted behavior or disobedience that the subject has displayed.
Crime	Crime refers to any action that violates criminal laws established by political authority. A crime in a nontechnical sense is an act that violates a very important political or moral command.
Manifest function	The intended and known consequences of one part of a sociocultural system is referred to as a manifest function.
Gender	Gender refers to socially defined behavior regarded as appropriate for the members of each
Melting pot	The melting pot is a metaphor for the way in which homogeneous societies develop, in which the ingredients in the pot (people of different cultures and religions) are combined so as to lose their discrete identities to some degree, yielding a final product which has a more uniform consistency and flavor, and which is quite different from the original inputs.
Innovations	A concept created by Robert Merton to describe the way norms assist in achieving goals are referred to as innovations.
Authority	Authority refers to power that is attached to a position that others perceive as legitimate.
Statistics	Statistics is a mathematical science pertaining to the collection, analysis, interpretation, and presentation of data. It is applicable to a wide variety of academic disciplines, from the physical and social sciences to the humanities; it is also used and misused for making informed decisions in all areas of business and government.
Parsons	Parsons was an advocate of "grand theory," an attempt to integrate all the social sciences into an overarching theoretical framework. His early work — The Structure of Social Action —reviewed the output of his great predecessors, especially Max Weber, Vilfredo Pareto, and Émile Durkheim, and attempted to derive from them a single "action theory" based on the assumptions that human action is voluntary, intentional, and symbolic.
Census	A census is the process of obtaining information about every member of a population. It can be contrasted with sampling in which information is only obtained from a subset of a population. As such it is a method used for accumulating statistical data, and it is also

Go to **Cram101.com** for the Practice Tests for this Chapter.

	vital to democracy.
Public defender	In the United States, a public defender is a lawyer whose duty is to provide legal counsel and representation to indigent defendants in criminal cases who are unable to pay for legal assistance.
Public policy	Public policy is a course of action or inaction chosen by public authorities to address a problem. Public policy is expressed in the body of laws, regulations, decisions and actions of government.
Community	Community refers to a group of people who share a common sense of identity and interact with one another on a sustained basis.
Vested interest	An expectation of private gain that often underlies the expressed interest in a public issue is a vested interest.
Interest group	Interest group refers to an organization that attempts to affect political decisions by supporting candidates sympathetic to their interests and by influencing those already in positions of authority.
Narcotic	A narcotic is an addictive drug, derived from opium, that reduces pain, induces sleep and may alter mood or behavior.
Deinstitutio-alization	Deinstitutionalization refers to the movement of mental patients out of hospitals and into the community.
Mental hospital	A medical institution specializing in providing inpatient care for psychological disorders is a psychiatric hospital or mental hospital.
Racial profiling	Racial profiling is inclusion of race in the profile of a persons considered likely to commit a particular crime or type of crime.
Crime prevention	Crime prevention is a term describing techniques used in reducing victimization as well as deterring crime and criminals. It is applied specifically to efforts made by governments to reduce crime and law enforcement and criminal justice.
Total institution	Total institution as defined by Erving Goffman, is an institution where all the aspects of life of individuals under the institution is controlled and regulated by the authorities of the organization. Total institutions are a social microcosmos dictated by hegemony and clear hierarchy.
Dominance	In animal colonies, a condition established by one animal over another by prevailing in an aggressive encounter between the two, is referred to as dominance.
Burglary	Burglary – also called breaking and entering or house breaking – is a crime related to theft. It typically involves someone breaking into a house with an intent to commit a crime.
Organization	In sociology organization is understood as planned, coordinated and purposeful action of human beings to construct or compile a common tangible or intangible product or service.
Brockway	Brockway was a penologist and is sometimes regarded as the "Father of prison reform" in the United States of America.
Penology	Penology comprises penitentiary science: that concerned with the processes devized and adopted for the punishment, repression, and prevention of crime, and the treatment of prisoners.
Deterrence	Deterrence is a theory from behavioral psychology about preventing or controlling actions or behavior through fear of punishment or retribution. This theory of criminology is shaping the criminal justice system of the United States and various other countries.
Variable	A characteristic that varies in value or magnitude along which an object, individual or group

	may be categorized, such as income or age, is referred to as a variable.
Conformity	Conformity is the act of consciously maintaining a certain degree of similarity (in clothing, manners, behaviors, etc.) to those in your general social circles, to those in authority, or to the general status quo. Usually, conformity implies a tendency to submit to others in thought and behavior other than simply clothing choice.
Religious movement	An association of people who join together to seek to spread a new religion or to promote a new interpretation of an existing religion is a religious movement.
Minnesota multiphasic personality inventory	The Minnesota Multiphasic Personality Inventory is the most frequently used personality test in the mental health fields. This assessment, or test, was designed to help identify personal, social, and behavioral problems in psychiatric patients.
Typology	Typology refers to the classification of observations in terms of their attributes on two or more variables. The classification of newspapers as liberal-urban, liberal-rural, conservative-urban, or conservative-rural would be an example of a typology.
Restitution	The law of restitution is the law of gains-based recovery. When a court orders restitution it orders the defendant to give up his gains to the claimant.
Geiger	Geiger is considered the founder of the concept of social stratification, using the concept of stratification (introduced by Edward Ross) for the analysis of social structures.
Attitude	Attitude refers to an enduring mental representation of a person, place, or thing that evokes an emotional response and related behavior.
Drug therapy	Control of psychological problems through drugs is referred to as drug therapy.
Manslaughter	Manslaughter refers to the killing of another person through gross negligence or without specific intent.
Liquor law	Liquor law is a term that refers to any legislation dealing with the abolishment, restriction, or regulation of the sale, consumption, and manufacture of alcoholic beverages.
Detention	Temporary care of a child alleged to be delinquent who requires secure custody in physically restricting facilities pending court disposition or execution of a court order is detention.
Murder	Murder is the unlawful, premeditated killing of a human being by another. The penalty for murder is usually either life imprisonment, or in jurisdictions with capital punishment, the death penalty.
Community service	Community service refers to service that a person performs for the benefit of his or her local community. People become involved in community service for a range of reasons, for some, it is an altruistic act, for others it is a punishment.
Gang	A gang is a group of individuals who share a common identity and, in current usage, engage in illegal activities. Historically the term referred to both criminal groups and ordinary groups of friends.
Compliance	Conforming behavior that occurs in response to direct social pressure is referred to as compliance.
Sexual assault	Sexual assault is any undesired physical contact of a sexual nature perpetrated against another person. While associated with rape, sexual assault is much broader and the specifics may vary according to social, political or legal definition.
Taylor	Taylor was an American engineer who sought to improve industrial efficiency. He was one of the intellectual leaders of the Efficiency Movement and his ideas, broadly conceived, were highly influential in the Progressive Era. During the latter part of his career he was a

Go to **Cram101.com** for the Practice Tests for this Chapter.

management consultant, and he is sometimes called "The Father of Scientific Management."

Informant	Someone well versed in the social phenomenon that you wish to study and who is willing to tell you what he or she knows about it is an informant.
Coping	Efforts to control, reduce, or learn to tolerate the threats that lead to stress is referred to as coping.
Technology	The application of logic, reason and knowledge to the problems of exploiting raw materials from the environment, is referred to as a technology.
Recidivism	The probability that those incarcerated and then released are likely to return to prison for the commission of new crimes is referred to as recidivism.
Control group	A group of people in an experiment who are not exposed to the experimental stimulus under study are referred to as a control group.
Child support	Income paid to a former spouse for support of dependent children following a divorce or separation is child support.
Motive	Motive refers to a hypothetical state within an organism that propels the organism toward a goal. In criminal law a motive is the cause that moves people and induce a certain action.
Sector	Sector refers to parts of the economy as judged by the economic activity that they constitute. For example agriculture, forestry, fishing and mining constitute the primary sector.
Electronic monitoring	Electronic monitoring refers to active monitoring systems consist of a radio transmitter worn by the offender that sends a continuous signal to the probation department computer, alerting officials if the offender leaves his or her place of confinement; passive systems employ computer-generated random phone calls that must be responded to in a certain period of time from a particular phone or other device.
Sanction	A punishment for nonconformity that reinforces socially approved forms of behavior is a sanction.
Hierarchy	A hierarchy is a system of ranking and organizing things or people, where each element of the system (except for the top element) is subordinate to a single other element. A hierarchy can link entities either directly or indirectly, and either vertically or horizontally. The only direct links in a hierarchy are to one's immediate superior, or to one of one's subordinates.
Mafia	Mafia refers to a method or system of patron-client relationships, and in Sicily it was a system dependent upon patronage and the ability of a man of respect to utilize violence when necessary.
Organized crime	Organized crime is crime carried out systematically by formal criminal organizations.
Aftercare	Transitional assistance to juveniles, equivalent to adult parole, to help youths adjust to community life is the aftercare. Aftercare programs encourage the development of social networks and activities to address emotional needs of recovering alcoholics and substance abusers.

Go to **Cram101.com** for the Practice Tests for this Chapter.

Crime	Crime refers to any action that violates criminal laws established by political authority. A crime in a nontechnical sense is an act that violates a very important political or moral command.
Society	A society is a grouping of individuals, which is characterized by common interest and may have distinctive culture and institutions.
Wilson	In The Declining Significance of Race: Blacks and Changing American Institutions Wilson argues that the significance of race is waning, and an African-American's class is comparatively more important in determining his or her life chances.
Murder	Murder is the unlawful, premeditated killing of a human being by another. The penalty for murder is usually either life imprisonment, or in jurisdictions with capital punishment, the death penalty.
Jurisdiction	Jurisdiction refers to every kind of judicial action; the authority of courts and judicial officers to decide cases.
Authority	Authority refers to power that is attached to a position that others perceive as legitimate.
Community	Community refers to a group of people who share a common sense of identity and interact with one another on a sustained basis.
Gang	A gang is a group of individuals who share a common identity and, in current usage, engage in illegal activities. Historically the term referred to both criminal groups and ordinary groups of friends.
Probation	Nonpunitive, legal disposition of juveniles emphasizing community treatment in which the juvenile is closely supervized by an officer of the court and must adhere to a strict set of rules to avoid incarceration is probation.
Mean	In statistics, mean has two related meanings: a)the average in ordinary English, which is also called the arithmetic mean (and is distinguished from the geometric mean or harmonic mean). The average is also called sample mean. b)the expected value of a random variable, which is also called the population mean.
Agribusiness	In agriculture, agribusiness is a generic term that refers to the various businesses involved in food production, including farming, seed supply, agrichemicals, farm machinery, wholesale and distribution, processing, marketing, and retail sales.
Brockway	Brockway was a penologist and is sometimes regarded as the "Father of prison reform" in the United States of America.
Determinate sentence	Sentence that specifies a fixed term of detention that must be served is referred to as the determinate sentence. A determinate sentence is only available for certain types of felony offenses.
Deterrence	Deterrence is a theory from behavioral psychology about preventing or controlling actions or behavior through fear of punishment or retribution. This theory of criminology is shaping the criminal justice system of the United States and various other countries.
Criminal justice	Criminal justice refers to the system used by government to maintain social control, enforce laws, and administer justice. Law enforcement (police), courts, and corrections are the primary agencies charged with these responsibilities.
Depression	In the field of psychiatry, the word depression can also have this meaning of low mood but more specifically refers to a mental illness when it has reached a severity and duration to warrant a diagnosis, whether there is an obvious situational cause or not.
Medical model	The application of the medical perspective in explaining and treating troublesome human behavior, is referred to as a medical model.

Social work	Social work is a helping profession focused on social change, problem solving in human relationships and the empowerment and liberation of people to enhance well-being.
Violent crime	A violent crime or crime of violence is a crime in which the offender uses or threatens to use violent force upon the victim. The United States Department of Justice Bureau of Justice Statistics (BJS) counts five categories of crime as violent crimes: murder, rape, robbery, aggravated assault, and simple assault.
Psychotherapy	Psychotherapy refers to a systematic interaction between a therapist and a client that brings psychological principles to bear on influencing the client's thoughts, feelings, or behavior to help that client overcome abnormal behavior or adjust to problems in living.
Indeterminate sentence	Indeterminate sentence does not specify the length of time the juvenile must be held; rather, correctional authorities decide when the juvenile is ready to return to society.
Minority group	A minority group or subordinate group is a sociological group that does not constitute a politically dominant plurality of the total population of a given society.
Tokenism	Tokenism refers to a policy or practice of limited inclusion of members of a minority group, usually creating a false appearance of inclusive practices, intentional or not. Typical examples in real life and fiction include purposely including a member of a minority race (such as a black character in a mainly white cast, or vice versa) into a group.
Recidivism	The probability that those incarcerated and then released are likely to return to prison for the commission of new crimes is referred to as recidivism.
Crime rate	Crime rate is a measure of the rate of occurrence of crimes committed in a given area and time. Most commonly, crime rate is given as the number of crimes committed among a given number of persons.
Government	A government is a body that has the authority to make and the power to enforce laws within a civil, corporate, religious, academic, or other organization or group.
Socioeconomic status	An overall rank based on characteristics such as education and occupation, used to describe people's positions in stratification systems is referred to as socioeconomic status.
Range	A measure of variability defined as the high score in a distribution minus the low score is referred to as a range.
Punishment	Punishment is the practice of imposing something unpleasant on a subject as a response to some unwanted behavior or disobedience that the subject has displayed.
Latent function	A latent function is a function that is neither recognized nor intended. A latent function of a behavior is not explicitly stated, recognized, or intended by the people involved.
Manifest function	The intended and known consequences of one part of a sociocultural system is referred to as a manifest function.
Subculture	A group within the broader society that has values, norms and lifestyle distinct from those of the majority, is referred to as a subculture.
Conformity	Conformity is the act of consciously maintaining a certain degree of similarity (in clothing, manners, behaviors, etc.) to those in your general social circles, to those in authority, or to the general status quo. Usually, conformity implies a tendency to submit to others in thought and behavior other than simply clothing choice.
Substance abuse	Substance abuse refers to the overindulgence in and dependence on a psychoactive leading to effects that are detrimental to the individual's physical health or mental health, or the welfare of others.
Technology	The application of logic, reason and knowledge to the problems of exploiting raw materials

50

Go to **Cram101.com** for the Practice Tests for this Chapter.

	from the environment, is referred to as a technology.
Sex offender	A sex offender is a person who has been criminally charged and convicted of, or has pled guilty to, a sex crime. As a label of identity it is used in criminal psychology.
Neighborhood	A neighborhood is a geographically localized community located within a larger city, town or suburb. Traditionally, a neighborhood is small enough that the neighbors are all able to know each other.
Public policy	Public policy is a course of action or inaction chosen by public authorities to address a problem. Public policy is expressed in the body of laws, regulations, decisions and actions of government.
American Civil Liberties Union	Lawsuits brought by the American Civil Liberties Union have been influential in the evolution of U.S. constitutional law. They provides legal assistance in cases in which it considers civil liberties to be at risk. Even when the they do not provide direct legal representation, it often submits amicus curiae briefs.
Social isolation	A type of loneliness that occurs when a person lacks a sense of integrated involvement. Being deprived of participation in a group or community involving companionship, shared interests, organized activities, and meaningful roles causes a person to feel is a social isolation.
Community service	Community service refers to service that a person performs for the benefit of his or her local community. People become involved in community service for a range of reasons, for some, it is an altruistic act, for others it is a punishment.
Restorative justice	Restorative justice is commonly known as a theory of criminal justice that focuses on crime as an act against another individual or community rather than the state. The victim plays a major role in the process and may receive some type of restitution from the offender.
Variable	A characteristic that varies in value or magnitude along which an object, individual or group may be categorized, such as income or age, is referred to as a variable.
Zero population growth	Zero Population Growth is a concept coined by American sociologist Kingsley Davis. It is a condition of demographic balance where population in a specified population neither grows nor declines.
Population growth	Population growth is change in population over time, and can be quantified as the change in the number of individuals in a population per unit time. The term population growth can technically refer to any species, but almost always refers to humans, and it is often used informally for the more specific demographic term population growth rate , and is often used to refer specifically to the growth of the population of the world.
Electronic monitoring	Electronic monitoring refers to active monitoring systems consist of a radio transmitter worn by the offender that sends a continuous signal to the probation department computer, alerting officials if the offender leaves his or her place of confinement; passive systems employ computer-generated random phone calls that must be responded to in a certain period of time from a particular phone or other device.
House arrest	House arrest refers to an offender is required to stay at home during specific periods of time; monitoring is done by random phone calls and visits or by electronic devices.
Coping	Efforts to control, reduce, or learn to tolerate the threats that lead to stress is referred to as coping.
Specific deterrence	Sending convicted offenders to secure incarceration facilities so that punishment is severe enough to convince offenders not to repeat their criminal activity is called specific deterrence.

Crime	Crime refers to any action that violates criminal laws established by political authority. A crime in a nontechnical sense is an act that violates a very important political or moral command.
Racism	Racism is a belief in the moral or biological superiority of one race or ethnic group over another or others.
Murder	Murder is the unlawful, premeditated killing of a human being by another. The penalty for murder is usually either life imprisonment, or in jurisdictions with capital punishment, the death penalty.
Consciousness	The awareness of the senzations, thoughts, and feelings being experienced at a given moment is referred to as consciousness.
Sexual abuse	Sexual abuse is defined by the forcing of undesired sexual acts by one person to another.
Sex offender	A sex offender is a person who has been criminally charged and convicted of, or has pled guilty to, a sex crime. As a label of identity it is used in criminal psychology.
Authority	Authority refers to power that is attached to a position that others perceive as legitimate.
Community	Community refers to a group of people who share a common sense of identity and interact with one another on a sustained basis.
Community service	Community service refers to service that a person performs for the benefit of his or her local community. People become involved in community service for a range of reasons, for some, it is an altruistic act, for others it is a punishment.
Restitution	The law of restitution is the law of gains-based recovery. When a court orders restitution it orders the defendant to give up his gains to the claimant.
Probation	Nonpunitive, legal disposition of juveniles emphasizing community treatment in which the juvenile is closely supervised by an officer of the court and must adhere to a strict set of rules to avoid incarceration is probation.
Mean	In statistics, mean has two related meanings: a)the average in ordinary English, which is also called the arithmetic mean (and is distinguished from the geometric mean or harmonic mean). The average is also called sample mean. b)the expected value of a random variable, which is also called the population mean.
Jurisdiction	Jurisdiction refers to every kind of judicial action; the authority of courts and judicial officers to decide cases.
Government	A government is a body that has the authority to make and the power to enforce laws within a civil, corporate, religious, academic, or other organization or group.
Due process	Basic constitutional principle based on the concept of the primacy of the individual and the complementary concept of limitation on governmental power; safeguards the individual from unfair state procedures in judicial or administrative proceedings; due process rights have been extended to juvenile trials.
Addiction	A pattern of behavior characterized by an overwhelming involvement with using a drug and securing its supply is defined as an addiction.
Child support	Income paid to a former spouse for support of dependent children following a divorce or separation is child support.
Society	A society is a grouping of individuals, which is characterized by common interest and may have distinctive culture and institutions.
Rape	Rape is the act of forcing penetrative sexual acts, against another's will through violence, force, threat of injury, or other duress, or where the victim is unable to decline, due to

	the effects of drugs or alcohol.
Violent crime	A violent crime or crime of violence is a crime in which the offender uses or threatens to use violent force upon the victim. The United States Department of Justice Bureau of Justice Statistics (BJS) counts five categories of crime as violent crimes: murder, rape, robbery, aggravated assault, and simple assault.
Social support	Social support is the physical and emotional comfort given to us by our family, friends, co-workers and others. It is knowing that we are part of a community of people who love and care for us, and value and think well of us.
Sector	Sector refers to parts of the economy as judged by the economic activity that they constitute. For example agriculture, forestry, fishing and mining constitute the primary sector.
Compliance	Conforming behavior that occurs in response to direct social pressure is referred to as compliance.
Range	A measure of variability defined as the high score in a distribution minus the low score is referred to as a range.
Glaser	Glaser, American sociologist and one of the founders of the grounded theory methodology. In 1999 Glaser founded the non-profit web based organization Grounded Theory Institute.
Aggravated Assault	Aggravated assault refers to an unlawful attack by one person upon another for the purpose of inflicting severe or aggravated bodily injury.
Robbery	The unlawful taking of, or the attempt to take something of value from another person or persons by using violence or the threat of violence, is referred to as a robbery.
Wilson	In The Declining Significance of Race: Blacks and Changing American Institutions Wilson argues that the significance of race is waning, and an African-American's class is comparatively more important in determining his or her life chances.
Recidivism	The probability that those incarcerated and then released are likely to return to prison for the commission of new crimes is referred to as recidivism.
Determinate sentence	Sentence that specifies a fixed term of detention that must be served is referred to as the determinate sentence. A determinate sentence is only available for certain types of felony offenses.
Criminal justice	Criminal justice refers to the system used by government to maintain social control, enforce laws, and administer justice. Law enforcement (police), courts, and corrections are the primary agencies charged with these responsibilities.
Electronic monitoring	Electronic monitoring refers to active monitoring systems consist of a radio transmitter worn by the offender that sends a continuous signal to the probation department computer, alerting officials if the offender leaves his or her place of confinement; passive systems employ computer-generated random phone calls that must be responded to in a certain period of time from a particular phone or other device.
House arrest	House arrest refers to an offender is required to stay at home during specific periods of time; monitoring is done by random phone calls and visits or by electronic devices.
Narcotic	A narcotic is an addictive drug, derived from opium, that reduces pain, induces sleep and may alter mood or behavior.
Felony	The term felony is used for very serious crimes, whereas misdemeanors are considered to be less serious offenses. It is a crime punishable by one or more years of imprisonment.
Substance abuse	Substance abuse refers to the overindulgence in and dependence on a psychoactive leading to

effects that are detrimental to the individual's physical health or mental health, or the welfare of others.

Detention	Temporary care of a child alleged to be delinquent who requires secure custody in physically restricting facilities pending court disposition or execution of a court order is detention.
Punishment	Punishment is the practice of imposing something unpleasant on a subject as a response to some unwanted behavior or disobedience that the subject has displayed.
Organized crime	Organized crime is crime carried out systematically by formal criminal organizations.
Disability	A physical or health condition that stigmatizes or causes discrimination, is referred to as a disability.
Informant	Someone well versed in the social phenomenon that you wish to study and who is willing to tell you what he or she knows about it is an informant.
Organization	In sociology organization is understood as planned, coordinated and purposeful action of human beings to construct or compile a common tangible or intangible product or service.
Sanction	A punishment for nonconformity that reinforces socially approved forms of behavior is a sanction.
Median	The number that falls halfway in a range of numbers, or the score below which are half the scores and above which are the other half is a median.
Victimizations	Victimizations refer to the number of people who are victims of criminal acts; young teens are fifteen times more likely than older adults to be victims of crimes.
Gang	A gang is a group of individuals who share a common identity and, in current usage, engage in illegal activities. Historically the term referred to both criminal groups and ordinary groups of friends.
Addict	A person with an overpowering physical or psychological need to continue taking a particular substance or drug is referred to as an addict.
Latent function	A latent function is a function that is neither recognized nor intended. A latent function of a behavior is not explicitly stated, recognized, or intended by the people involved.
Social work	Social work is a helping profession focused on social change, problem solving in human relationships and the empowerment and liberation of people to enhance well-being.
Mental hospital	A medical institution specializing in providing inpatient care for psychological disorders is a psychiatric hospital or mental hospital.
Deterrence	Deterrence is a theory from behavioral psychology about preventing or controlling actions or behavior through fear of punishment or retribution. This theory of criminology is shaping the criminal justice system of the United States and various other countries.
Charles Manson	Charles Manson is an American convict and career criminal, most known for his participation in the Tate-LaBianca murders of the late 1960s.
Serial killer	A serial killer is someone who kills on at least three occasions, taking breaks between murders. The crimes committed are a result of a compulsion that may have roots in the killer's (often dysfunctional) youth and psychopathological disorders.
Capital punishment	Use of the death penalty to punish offenders is called capital punishment.
Social order	Social order refers to a set of linked social structures, social institutions and social practices which conserve, maintain and enforce "normal" ways of relating and behaving.
Scientific	Scientific method is a body of techniques for investigating phenomena and acquiring new

Go to **Cram101.com** for the Practice Tests for this Chapter.

method	knowledge, as well as for correcting and integrating previous knowledge. It is based on gathering observable, empirical, measurable evidence, subject to the principles of reasoning.
Technology	The application of logic, reason and knowledge to the problems of exploiting raw materials from the environment, is referred to as a technology.
Validity	The degree to which a measurement instrument measures what it is intended to measure is referred to as validity.
Wright	Wright is an American sociologist. His work is concerned mainly with the study of social classes, and in particular with the task of providing an update to the Marxist concept of class. Wright has stressed the importance of the control of the means of production in defining 'class', while at the same trying to account for the situation of skilled employees, taking inspiration from Weberian accounts of authority.
Aggregate	Aggregate refers to a collection of people who happen to be in the same place at the same time.
Attitude	Attitude refers to an enduring mental representation of a person, place, or thing that evokes an emotional response and related behavior.
Empirical research	Empirical research is any research that bases its findings on direct or indirect observation as its test of reality. Such research may also be conducted according to hypothetico-deductive procedures, such as those developed from the work of R. A. Fisher.
Reliability	Reliability refers to the degree to which a measurement instrument gives the same results with repeated measurements.
Group therapy	Group therapy is a form of psychotherapy during which one or several therapists treat a small group of clients together as a group. This may be more cost effective than individual therapy, and possibly even more productive.
Neighborhood	A neighborhood is a geographically localized community located within a larger city, town or suburb. Traditionally, a neighborhood is small enough that the neighbors are all able to know each other.
Coleman	Coleman was a sociological theorist, who studied the sociology of education, public policy, and was one of the earliest users of the term "social capital". His Foundations of Social Theory stands as one of the most important sociological contributions of the late-20th century.
Mandatory sentence	A criminal sentence that is defined by a statutory requirement that states the penalty to be set for all cases of a specific offense is called a mandatory sentence.
Probable cause	Reasonable ground to believe the existence of facts that an offense was committed and that the accused committed that offense is called probable cause.
Cocaine	Cocaine is a crystalline tropane alkaloid that is obtained from the leaves of the coca plant. It is a stimulant of the central nervous system and an appetite suppressant, creating what has been described as a euphoric sense of happiness and increased energy.

60

Go to **Cram101.com** for the Practice Tests for this Chapter.

Jurisdiction	Jurisdiction refers to every kind of judicial action; the authority of courts and judicial officers to decide cases.
Aftercare	Transitional assistance to juveniles, equivalent to adult parole, to help youths adjust to community life is the aftercare. Aftercare programs encourage the development of social networks and activities to address emotional needs of recovering alcoholics and substance abusers.
Probation	Nonpunitive, legal disposition of juveniles emphasizing community treatment in which the juvenile is closely supervized by an officer of the court and must adhere to a strict set of rules to avoid incarceration is probation.
Felony	The term felony is used for very serious crimes, whereas misdemeanors are considered to be less serious offenses. It is a crime punishable by one or more years of imprisonment.
Organization	In sociology organization is understood as planned, coordinated and purposeful action of human beings to construct or compile a common tangible or intangible product or service.
Compliance	Conforming behavior that occurs in response to direct social pressure is referred to as compliance.
Community	Community refers to a group of people who share a common sense of identity and interact with one another on a sustained basis.
Society	A society is a grouping of individuals, which is characterized by common interest and may have distinctive culture and institutions.
Crime	Crime refers to any action that violates criminal laws established by political authority. A crime in a nontechnical sense is an act that violates a very important political or moral command.
Sanction	A punishment for nonconformity that reinforces socially approved forms of behavior is a sanction.
Electronic monitoring	Electronic monitoring refers to active monitoring systems consist of a radio transmitter worn by the offender that sends a continuous signal to the probation department computer, alerting officials if the offender leaves his or her place of confinement; passive systems employ computer-generated random phone calls that must be responded to in a certain period of time from a particular phone or other device.
Recidivism	The probability that those incarcerated and then released are likely to return to prison for the commission of new crimes is referred to as recidivism.
Community service	Community service refers to service that a person performs for the benefit of his or her local community. People become involved in community service for a range of reasons, for some, it is an altruistic act, for others it is a punishment.
Punishment	Punishment is the practice of imposing something unpleasant on a subject as a response to some unwanted behavior or disobedience that the subject has displayed.
Reinforcement	A stimulus that follows a response and increases the frequency of the response is a reinforcement.
Restitution	The law of restitution is the law of gains-based recovery. When a court orders restitution it orders the defendant to give up his gains to the claimant.
Range	A measure of variability defined as the high score in a distribution minus the low score is referred to as a range.
Professional-zation	The social process through which an occupation acquires the cultural and structural characteristics of a profession is professionalization.

Medical model	The application of the medical perspective in explaining and treating troublesome human behavior, is referred to as a medical model.
Criminal justice	Criminal justice refers to the system used by government to maintain social control, enforce laws, and administer justice. Law enforcement (police), courts, and corrections are the primary agencies charged with these responsibilities.
Government	A government is a body that has the authority to make and the power to enforce laws within a civil, corporate, religious, academic, or other organization or group.
Mean	In statistics, mean has two related meanings: a)the average in ordinary English, which is also called the arithmetic mean (and is distinguished from the geometric mean or harmonic mean). The average is also called sample mean. b)the expected value of a random variable, which is also called the population mean.
Criminal law	Criminal law (also known as penal law) is the body of statutory and common law that deals with crime and the legal punishment of criminal offenses. There are four theories of criminal justice: punishment, deterrence, incapacitation, and rehabilitation.
Statistics	Statistics is a mathematical science pertaining to the collection, analysis, interpretation, and presentation of data. It is applicable to a wide variety of academic disciplines, from the physical and social sciences to the humanities; it is also used and misused for making informed decisions in all areas of business and government.
Attitude	Attitude refers to an enduring mental representation of a person, place, or thing that evokes an emotional response and related behavior.
Alienation	In sociology and critical social theory, alienation refers to the individual's estrangement from traditional community and others in general.
Validity	The degree to which a measurement instrument measures what it is intended to measure is referred to as validity.
Minnesota multiphasic personality inventory	The Minnesota Multiphasic Personality Inventory is the most frequently used personality test in the mental health fields. This assessment, or test, was designed to help identify personal, social, and behavioral problems in psychiatric patients.
Sexual assault	Sexual assault is any undesired physical contact of a sexual nature perpetrated against another person. While associated with rape, sexual assault is much broader and the specifics may vary according to social, political or legal definition.
Sex offender	A sex offender is a person who has been criminally charged and convicted of, or has pled guilty to, a sex crime. As a label of identity it is used in criminal psychology.
Rape	Rape is the act of forcing penetrative sexual acts, against another's will through violence, force, threat of injury, or other duress, or where the victim is unable to decline, due to the effects of drugs or alcohol.
Criminology	Criminology refers to the systematic study of crime and the criminal justice system, including the police, courts, and prisons.
Gang	A gang is a group of individuals who share a common identity and, in current usage, engage in illegal activities. Historically the term referred to both criminal groups and ordinary groups of friends.
Neighborhood	A neighborhood is a geographically localized community located within a larger city, town or suburb. Traditionally, a neighborhood is small enough that the neighbors are all able to know each other.
Immunity	Immunity confers a status on a person or body that places him/her/it above the law and makes

	that person or body free from otherwise legal obligations such as, for example, liability for torts or damages or prosecution under criminal law for criminal acts.
Embezzlement	Embezzlement is the fraudulent appropriation by a person to his own use of property or money entrusted to that person's care but owned by someone else.
Authority	Authority refers to power that is attached to a position that others perceive as legitimate.
Robbery	The unlawful taking of, or the attempt to take something of value from another person or persons by using violence or the threat of violence, is referred to as a robbery.
Civil rights	Civil rights are the protections and privileges of personal liberty given to all citizens by law. Civil rights are rights that are bestowed by nations on those within their territorial boundaries.
Omission	Omission is, in Catholic teaching, the failure to do something one can and ought to do. If this happens advertently and freely a sin is committed. The degree of guilt incurred by an omission is measured like that attaching to sins of commission, by the dignity of the virtue and the magnitude of the precept to which the omission is opposed as well as the amount of deliberation.
Consensus	Agreement on basic social values by the members of a group or society is referred to as a consensus.
Edwin Sutherland	Edwin Sutherland (1893–1950) is considered to be one of the most influential criminologists of the twentieth century. He is best known for defining differential association which is a general theory of crime and delinquency that explains how deviants come to learn the motivations and the technical knowledge for deviant or criminal activity.
Technology	The application of logic, reason and knowledge to the problems of exploiting raw materials from the environment, is referred to as a technology.
Polygraph	Polygraph refers to a machine that monitors changes physiological thought to be influenced by emotional states and it is used by examiners to try to determine if someone is lying.
Strauss	Strauss was an American sociologist, who worked the field of medical sociology. Strauss is best known for his work on the methodology in qualitative research and in particular for the development of grounded theory, a general methodology he established together with Barney Glaser in the 1960s.
Random assignment	Assignment of participants to experimental and control groups by chance is referred to as a random assignment.
Numbers game	The Numbers Game or Policy Racket is an illegal lottery played mostly in poor neighborhoods in U.S. cities, wherein the bettor attempts to pick three or four digits to match those that will be randomly drawn the following day.
Empathy	Empathy is commonly defined as one's ability to recognize, perceive and directly experientially feel the emotion of another. As the states of mind, beliefs, and desires of others are intertwined with their emotions, one with empathy for another may often be able to more effectively divine another's modes of thought and mood.
Immigration	Although human migration has existed for hundreds of thousands of years, immigration in the modern sense refers to movement of people from one nation-state to another, where they are not citizens.
Murder	Murder is the unlawful, premeditated killing of a human being by another. The penalty for murder is usually either life imprisonment, or in jurisdictions with capital punishment, the death penalty.
Mafia	Mafia refers to a method or system of patron-client relationships, and in Sicily it was a

	system dependent upon patronage and the ability of a man of respect to utilize violence when necessary.
Ghetto	A ghetto is an area where people from a specific racial or ethnic background or united in a given culture or religion live as a group, voluntarily or involuntarily, in milder or stricter seclusion.
Role conflict	Role conflict is a special form of social conflict that takes place when one is forced to take on two different and incompatible roles at the same time.
Motive	Motive refers to a hypothetical state within an organism that propels the organism toward a goal. In criminal law a motive is the cause that moves people and induce a certain action.
Prestige	Prestige refers to social respect accorded to an individual or group because of the status of their position.
Aggregate	Aggregate refers to a collection of people who happen to be in the same place at the same time.
Entitlement	The feeling that one has a right to certain privileges and that specific rewards should be forthcoming by virtue of what they have done or who they are is an entitlement.
Cultural diversity	Cultural diversity is the variety of human societies or cultures in a specific region, or in the world as a whole.

Go to **Cram101.com** for the Practice Tests for this Chapter.

Community	Community refers to a group of people who share a common sense of identity and interact with one another on a sustained basis.
Probation	Nonpunitive, legal disposition of juveniles emphasizing community treatment in which the juvenile is closely supervised by an officer of the court and must adhere to a strict set of rules to avoid incarceration is probation.
Jurisdiction	Jurisdiction refers to every kind of judicial action; the authority of courts and judicial officers to decide cases.
Society	A society is a grouping of individuals, which is characterized by common interest and may have distinctive culture and institutions.
Gang	A gang is a group of individuals who share a common identity and, in current usage, engage in illegal activities. Historically the term referred to both criminal groups and ordinary groups of friends.
Neighborhood	A neighborhood is a geographically localized community located within a larger city, town or suburb. Traditionally, a neighborhood is small enough that the neighbors are all able to know each other.
Burnout	A feeling of overload, including mental and physical exhaustion, that usually results from a gradual accumulation of everyday stresses is defined as burnout.
Criminal justice	Criminal justice refers to the system used by government to maintain social control, enforce laws, and administer justice. Law enforcement (police), courts, and corrections are the primary agencies charged with these responsibilities.
Social work	Social work is a helping profession focused on social change, problem solving in human relationships and the empowerment and liberation of people to enhance well-being.
Reform movement	A reform movement is a kind of social movement that aims to make gradual change, or change in certain aspects of the society rather than rapid or fundamental changes.
Criminologist	A criminologist is often defined as someone who studies the aetiology of crime, criminal behavior, types of crime, and social, cultural and media reactions to crime.
Minnesota multiphasic personality inventory	The Minnesota Multiphasic Personality Inventory is the most frequently used personality test in the mental health fields. This assessment, or test, was designed to help identify personal, social, and behavioral problems in psychiatric patients.
Reliability	Reliability refers to the degree to which a measurement instrument gives the same results with repeated measurements.
Typology	Typology refers to the classification of observations in terms of their attributes on two or more variables. The classification of newspapers as liberal-urban, liberal-rural, conservative-urban, or conservative-rural would be an example of a typology.
Parsons	Parsons was an advocate of "grand theory," an attempt to integrate all the social sciences into an overarching theoretical framework. His early work — The Structure of Social Action —reviewed the output of his great predecessors, especially Max Weber, Vilfredo Pareto, and Émile Durkheim, and attempted to derive from them a single "action theory" based on the assumptions that human action is voluntary, intentional, and symbolic.
Life history	Life history refers to a variety of methods and techniques that are used for conducting qualitative interviews. The method was first used when interviewing indigenous peoples of the Americas.
Authority	Authority refers to power that is attached to a position that others perceive as legitimate.

Go to **Cram101.com** for the Practice Tests for this Chapter.

Deterrence	Deterrence is a theory from behavioral psychology about preventing or controlling actions or behavior through fear of punishment or retribution. This theory of criminology is shaping the criminal justice system of the United States and various other countries.
Punishment	Punishment is the practice of imposing something unpleasant on a subject as a response to some unwanted behavior or disobedience that the subject has displayed.
Crime	Crime refers to any action that violates criminal laws established by political authority. A crime in a nontechnical sense is an act that violates a very important political or moral command.
Government	A government is a body that has the authority to make and the power to enforce laws within a civil, corporate, religious, academic, or other organization or group.
Substance abuse	Substance abuse refers to the overindulgence in and dependence on a psychoactive leading to effects that are detrimental to the individual's physical health or mental health, or the welfare of others.
Felony	The term felony is used for very serious crimes, whereas misdemeanors are considered to be less serious offenses. It is a crime punishable by one or more years of imprisonment.
Criminal law	Criminal law (also known as penal law) is the body of statutory and common law that deals with crime and the legal punishment of criminal offenses. There are four theories of criminal justice: punishment, deterrence, incapacitation, and rehabilitation.
Mean	In statistics, mean has two related meanings: a)the average in ordinary English, which is also called the arithmetic mean (and is distinguished from the geometric mean or harmonic mean). The average is also called sample mean. b)the expected value of a random variable, which is also called the population mean.
Range	A measure of variability defined as the high score in a distribution minus the low score is referred to as a range.
Frequency	In statistics the frequency of an event i is the number n_i of times the event occurred in the experiment or the study.
Recidivism	The probability that those incarcerated and then released are likely to return to prison for the commission of new crimes is referred to as recidivism.
Sanction	A punishment for nonconformity that reinforces socially approved forms of behavior is a sanction.
Crime rate	Crime rate is a measure of the rate of occurrence of crimes committed in a given area and time. Most commonly, crime rate is given as the number of crimes committed among a given number of persons.
Preventive detention	Keeping the accused in custody prior to trial because the accused is suspected of being a danger to the community is called preventive detention.
Detention	Temporary care of a child alleged to be delinquent who requires secure custody in physically restricting facilities pending court disposition or execution of a court order is detention.
Variable	A characteristic that varies in value or magnitude along which an object, individual or group may be categorized, such as income or age, is referred to as a variable.
Sex offender	A sex offender is a person who has been criminally charged and convicted of, or has pled guilty to, a sex crime. As a label of identity it is used in criminal psychology.
Adaptation	Adaptation refers to the ability of a sociocultural system to change with the demands of a changing physical or social environment.
Electronic	Electronic monitoring refers to active monitoring systems consist of a radio transmitter worn

Go to **Cram101.com** for the Practice Tests for this Chapter.

monitoring	by the offender that sends a continuous signal to the probation department computer, alerting officials if the offender leaves his or her place of confinement; passive systems employ computer-generated random phone calls that must be responded to in a certain period of time from a particular phone or other device.
House arrest	House arrest refers to an offender is required to stay at home during specific periods of time; monitoring is done by random phone calls and visits or by electronic devices.
Violent crime	A violent crime or crime of violence is a crime in which the offender uses or threatens to use violent force upon the victim. The United States Department of Justice Bureau of Justice Statistics (BJS) counts five categories of crime as violent crimes: murder, rape, robbery, aggravated assault, and simple assault.
Technology	The application of logic, reason and knowledge to the problems of exploiting raw materials from the environment, is referred to as a technology.
Battery	In many common law jurisdictions, the crime of battery involves an injury or other contact upon the person of another in a manner likely to cause bodily harm.
Wilson	In The Declining Significance of Race: Blacks and Changing American Institutions Wilson argues that the significance of race is waning, and an African-American's class is comparatively more important in determining his or her life chances.
Statistics	Statistics is a mathematical science pertaining to the collection, analysis, interpretation, and presentation of data. It is applicable to a wide variety of academic disciplines, from the physical and social sciences to the humanities; it is also used and misused for making informed decisions in all areas of business and government.
Statutory law	Statutory law is written law set down by a legislature or other governing authority such as the executive branch of government in response to a perceived need to clarify the functioning of government, improve civil order, answer a public need, to codify existing law, or for an individual or company to obtain special treatment.
Immigration	Although human migration has existed for hundreds of thousands of years, immigration in the modern sense refers to movement of people from one nation-state to another, where they are not citizens.
Wright	Wright is an American sociologist. His work is concerned mainly with the study of social classes, and in particular with the task of providing an update to the Marxist concept of class. Wright has stressed the importance of the control of the means of production in defining 'class', while at the same trying to account for the situation of skilled employees, taking inspiration from Weberian accounts of authority.
Crime prevention	Crime prevention is a term describing techniques used in reducing victimization as well as deterring crime and criminals. It is applied specifically to efforts made by governments to reduce crime and law enforcement and criminal justice.
Organized crime	Organized crime is crime carried out systematically by formal criminal organizations.
Community service	Community service refers to service that a person performs for the benefit of his or her local community. People become involved in community service for a range of reasons, for some, it is an altruistic act, for others it is a punishment.
Role performance	The actual behavior of people who occupy a status is referred to as a role performance.
Gender	Gender refers to socially defined behavior regarded as appropriate for the members of each
Depersonaliz-tion	Depersonalization refers to the perceptual experience of one's body or surroundings becoming distorted or unreal.
Role conflict	Role conflict is a special form of social conflict that takes place when one is forced to

Go to **Cram101.com** for the Practice Tests for this Chapter.

take on two different and incompatible roles at the same time.

Divorce rate	The number of divorces over a specified period per specified popularion.The divorce rate is often calculated per 1,000 population or by estimating the proportion of all marriages that are expected to end in divorce.
Alienation	In sociology and critical social theory, alienation refers to the individual's estrangement from traditional community and others in general.
Depression	In the field of psychiatry, the word depression can also have this meaning of low mood but more specifically refers to a mental illness when it has reached a severity and duration to warrant a diagnosis, whether there is an obvious situational cause or not.
Attitude	Attitude refers to an enduring mental representation of a person, place, or thing that evokes an emotional response and related behavior.
Coping	Efforts to control, reduce, or learn to tolerate the threats that lead to stress is referred to as coping.
Mills	Mills is best remembered for studying the structure of Power in the U.S. in his book, The Power Elite. Mills was concerned with the responsibilities of intellectuals in post-World War II society, and advocated relevance and engagement over disinterested academic observation, as a "public intelligence apparatus" in challenging the crackpot policies of these institutional elite in the "Big Three", the economic, political and military.
Organization	In sociology organization is understood as planned, coordinated and purposeful action of human beings to construct or compile a common tangible or intangible product or service.
Hierarchy	A hierarchy is a system of ranking and organizing things or people, where each element of the system (except for the top element) is subordinate to a single other element. A hierarchy can link entities either directly or indirectly, and either vertically or horizontally. The only direct links in a hierarchy are to one's immediate superior, or to one of one's subordinates.
Aggravated Assault	Aggravated assault refers to an unlawful attack by one person upon another for the purpose of inflicting severe or aggravated bodily injury.
Murder	Murder is the unlawful, premeditated killing of a human being by another. The penalty for murder is usually either life imprisonment, or in jurisdictions with capital punishment, the death penalty.
Rape	Rape is the act of forcing penetrative sexual acts, against another's will through violence, force, threat of injury, or other duress, or where the victim is unable to decline, due to the effects of drugs or alcohol.
Immunity	Immunity confers a status on a person or body that places him/her/it above the law and makes that person or body free from otherwise legal obligations such as, for example, liability for torts or damages or prosecution under criminal law for criminal acts.
Civil rights	Civil rights are the protections and privileges of personal liberty given to all citizens by law. Civil rights are rights that are bestowed by nations on those within their territorial boundaries.
Comparative criminology	The systematic comparison of crime, law, and social control in two or more cultures is referred to as comparative criminology.
Criminology	Criminology refers to the systematic study of crime and the criminal justice system, including the police, courts, and prisons.

Go to **Cram101.com** for the Practice Tests for this Chapter.

Government	A government is a body that has the authority to make and the power to enforce laws within a civil, corporate, religious, academic, or other organization or group.
Murder	Murder is the unlawful, premeditated killing of a human being by another. The penalty for murder is usually either life imprisonment, or in jurisdictions with capital punishment, the death penalty.
Criminal justice	Criminal justice refers to the system used by government to maintain social control, enforce laws, and administer justice. Law enforcement (police), courts, and corrections are the primary agencies charged with these responsibilities.
Criminologist	A criminologist is often defined as someone who studies the aetiology of crime, criminal behavior, types of crime, and social, cultural and media reactions to crime.
Crime	Crime refers to any action that violates criminal laws established by political authority. A crime in a nontechnical sense is an act that violates a very important political or moral command.
Societal reaction	Part of the process of deviance by which society labels primary deviants, thus giving them an identity that leads them to act in expected ways, causing secondary deviance, is referred to as a societal reaction.
Criminology	Criminology refers to the systematic study of crime and the criminal justice system, including the police, courts, and prisons.
Motive	Motive refers to a hypothetical state within an organism that propels the organism toward a goal. In criminal law a motive is the cause that moves people and induce a certain action.
Attention Deficit Hyperactivity Disorder	Attention deficit hyperactivity disorder is a learning disability marked by inattention, impulsiveness, a low tolerance for frustration, and a great deal of inappropriate activity.
Juvenile court	Court that has original jurisdiction over persons defined by statute as juveniles and alleged to be delinquents, status offenders, or dependents is called juvenile court.
Labeling theory	A social theory that holds that society's reaction to certain behaviors is a major factor in defining the self as deviant is labeling theory.
Labeling	Labeling is defining or describing a person in terms of his or her behavior. The term is often used in sociology to describe human interaction, control and identification of deviant behavior.
Mean	In statistics, mean has two related meanings: a)the average in ordinary English, which is also called the arithmetic mean (and is distinguished from the geometric mean or harmonic mean). The average is also called sample mean. b)the expected value of a random variable, which is also called the population mean.
Social isolation	A type of loneliness that occurs when a person lacks a sense of integrated involvement. Being deprived of participation in a group or community involving companionship, shared interests, organized activities, and meaningful roles causes a person to feel is a social isolation.
Authority	Authority refers to power that is attached to a position that others perceive as legitimate.
Criminal organization	A criminal organization is a group run by criminals, most commonly for the purpose of generating a monetary profit. They are usually involved with drugs, prostitution and human trafficking, money laundering, governmental corruption and black marketeering.
Organization	In sociology organization is understood as planned, coordinated and purposeful action of human beings to construct or compile a common tangible or intangible product or service.

Gang	A gang is a group of individuals who share a common identity and, in current usage, engage in illegal activities. Historically the term referred to both criminal groups and ordinary groups of friends.
Subculture	A group within the broader society that has values, norms and lifestyle distinct from those of the majority, is referred to as a subculture.
Recidivism	The probability that those incarcerated and then released are likely to return to prison for the commission of new crimes is referred to as recidivism.
Probation	Nonpunitive, legal disposition of juveniles emphasizing community treatment in which the juvenile is closely supervized by an officer of the court and must adhere to a strict set of rules to avoid incarceration is probation.
Burglary	Burglary – also called breaking and entering or house breaking – is a crime related to theft. It typically involves someone breaking into a house with an intent to commit a crime.
Deviant behavior	Deviant behavior is behavior that is a recognized violation of social norms. Formal and informal social controls attempt to prevent and minimize deviance. One such control is through the medicalization of deviance.
Social status	Social status refers to a position in a social relationship, a characteristic that locates individuals in relation to other people and sets of role expectations.
Conformity	Conformity is the act of consciously maintaining a certain degree of similarity (in clothing, manners, behaviors, etc.) to those in your general social circles, to those in authority, or to the general status quo. Usually, conformity implies a tendency to submit to others in thought and behavior other than simply clothing choice.
Neighborhood	A neighborhood is a geographically localized community located within a larger city, town or suburb. Traditionally, a neighborhood is small enough that the neighbors are all able to know each other.
Social class	A category of people who occupy a similar position in relation to the means through which goods and services are produced in a society is a social class.
Crime rate	Crime rate is a measure of the rate of occurrence of crimes committed in a given area and time. Most commonly, crime rate is given as the number of crimes committed among a given number of persons.
Cesare Lombroso	Cesare Lombroso was a historical figure in modern criminology, and the founder of the Italian School of Positivist Criminology. He rejected the established Classical School, which held that crime was a characteristic trait of human nature.
Abnormal behavior	Actions, thoughts, and feelings that are harmful to the person or to others is referred to as an abnormal behavior.
Antidepressant	An antidepressant is a medication designed to treat or alleviate the symptoms of clinical depression. Some, notably the tricyclics, are commonly used off-label in the treatment of neuropathic pain, whether or not the patient is depressed. Smaller doses are generally used for this purpose, and they often take effect more quickly.
Sex offender	A sex offender is a person who has been criminally charged and convicted of, or has pled guilty to, a sex crime. As a label of identity it is used in criminal psychology.
Drug therapy	Control of psychological problems through drugs is referred to as drug therapy.
Compulsion	An apparently irresistible urge to repeat an act or engage in ritualistic behavior, often despite negative consequences is referred to as a compulsion.
Castration	Castration is any action, surgical, chemical, or otherwise, by which a biological male loses

use of the testes. A temporary chemical castration has been studied and developed as a preventive measure and punishment for several repeated sex crimes such as rape or other sexually related violence.

Jurisdiction	Jurisdiction refers to every kind of judicial action; the authority of courts and judicial officers to decide cases.
Violent crime	A violent crime or crime of violence is a crime in which the offender uses or threatens to use violent force upon the victim. The United States Department of Justice Bureau of Justice Statistics (BJS) counts five categories of crime as violent crimes: murder, rape, robbery, aggravated assault, and simple assault.
Community	Community refers to a group of people who share a common sense of identity and interact with one another on a sustained basis.
Social learning theory	A theory emphasizing that boys develop maleness and girls develop femaleness through exposure to scores of influence-including parents, peers, television, and schools-that teach them what it means to be a man or a woman in their culture, is referred to as a social learning theory.
Social learning	The process through which we acquire new information, forms of behavior, or attitudes exclusively or primarily in a social group, is referred to as a social learning.
Technology	The application of logic, reason and knowledge to the problems of exploiting raw materials from the environment, is referred to as a technology.
Adolescence	Adolescence is the transitional stage of human development in which a juvenile matures into an adult. This transition involves biological (i.e. pubertal), social, and psychological changes, though the biological ones are the easiest to measure objectively.
Group therapy	Group therapy is a form of psychotherapy during which one or several therapists treat a small group of clients together as a group. This may be more cost effective than individual therapy, and possibly even more productive.
Society	A society is a grouping of individuals, which is characterized by common interest and may have distinctive culture and institutions.
Social support	Social support is the physical and emotional comfort given to us by our family, friends, co-workers and others. It is knowing that we are part of a community of people who love and care for us, and value and think well of us.
Community service	Community service refers to service that a person performs for the benefit of his or her local community. People become involved in community service for a range of reasons, for some, it is an altruistic act, for others it is a punishment.
Gender	Gender refers to socially defined behavior regarded as appropriate for the members of each
Bias	A bias is a prejudice in a general or specific sense, usually in the sense for having a preference to one particular point of view or ideological perspective.
Reinforcement	A stimulus that follows a response and increases the frequency of the response is a reinforcement.
Social group	A group that consists of two or more people who interact frequently and share a common identity and a feeling of interdependence, is referred to as a social group.
Socialization	Socialization refers to the lifelong processes through which humans develop an awareness of social norms and values, and achieve a distinct sense of self.
Social structure	The term social structure, used in a general sense, refers to entities or groups in definite relation to each other, to relatively enduring patterns of behavior and relationship within social systems, or to social institutions and norms becoming embedded into social systems in

Go to **Cram101.com** for the Practice Tests for this Chapter.

such a way that they shape the behavior of actors within those social systems.

Differential Association	In criminology, Differential Association is a theory developed by Edwin Sutherland proposing that through interaction with others, individuals learn the values, attitudes, techniques, and motives for criminal behavior.
Social Control Theory	In criminology, Social Control Theory as represented in the work of Travis Hirschi fits into the Positivist School, Neo-Classical School, and, later, Right Realism. It proposes that exploiting the process of socialization and social learning builds self-control and reduces the inclination to indulge in behavior recognized as antisocial.
Social control	A social mechanism that regulates individual and group behavior through sanctions and rewards is a social control.
Control theory	A theory that views crime as the outcome of an imbalance between impulses toward criminal activity and controls that deter it is referred to as control theory. Control theorists hold that criminals are rational beings who will act to maximize their own reward.
Anomie Theory	Merton's theory of deviance which holds that many forms of deviance are caused by a disjunction between society's goals and the approved means to achieve these goal is referred to as anomie theory.
Anomie	Durkheim's designation for a condition in which social control becomes ineffective as a result of the loss of shared values and a sense of purpose in society is defined as anomie.
Edwin Sutherland	Edwin Sutherland (1893–1950) is considered to be one of the most influential criminologists of the twentieth century. He is best known for defining differential association which is a general theory of crime and delinquency that explains how deviants come to learn the motivations and the technical knowledge for deviant or criminal activity.
Cultural transmission	Cultural transmission refers to the socialization process whereby the norms and values of the group are passed on through learning from one generation to the next generation.
Social interaction	Social interaction is a dynamic, changing sequence of social actions between individuals (or groups) who modify their actions and reactions due to the actions by their interaction partner(s). In other words they are events in which people attach meaning to a situation, interpret what others are meaning, and respond accordingly.
Frequency	In statistics the frequency of an event i is the number n_i of times the event occurred in the experiment or the study.
Prestige	Prestige refers to social respect accorded to an individual or group because of the status of their position.
Rationalization	Rationalization is the process whereby an increasing number of social actions and interactions become based on considerations of efficiency or calculation rather than on motivations derived from custom, tradition, or emotion.
Neutralization theory	Gresham Sykes and David Matza's neutralization theory explains how deviants justified their deviant behaviors by adjusting the definitions of their actions and by explaining to themselves and others the lack of guilt of their actions in particular situations.
Adaptation	Adaptation refers to the ability of a sociocultural system to change with the demands of a changing physical or social environment.
Normlessness	Emile Durkheim described anomie which is state of relative normlessness or a state in which norms have been eroded.
Norm	In sociology, a norm, or social norm, is a rule that is socially enforced. Social sanctioning is what distinguishes norms from other cultural products such as meaning and values.

Durkheim	Durkheim sought to create one of the first scientific approaches to social phenomena. Along with Herbert Spencer, Durkheim was one of the first people to explain the existence and quality of different parts of a society by reference to what function they served in keeping the society healthy and balanced—a position that would come to be known as functionalism.
Merton	Merton coined the phrase "self-fulfilling prophecy." He also coined many other phrases that have gone into everyday use, such as "role model" and "unintended consequences".
Mode	In statistics, mode means the most frequent value assumed by a random variable, or occurring in a sampling of a random variable.
Rebellion	A rebellion is, in the most general sense, a refusal to accept authority. It may therefore be seen as encompassing a range of behaviors from civil disobedience to a violent organized attempt to destroy established authority. It is often used in reference to armed resistance against an established government, but can also refer to mass nonviolent resistance movements.
Larceny	Larceny is the trespassory taking and asportation of the (tangible) personal property of another with the intent to deprive him or her of it permanently.
Embezzlement	Embezzlement is the fraudulent appropriation by a person to his own use of property or money entrusted to that person's care but owned by someone else.
Aggravated Assault	Aggravated assault refers to an unlawful attack by one person upon another for the purpose of inflicting severe or aggravated bodily injury.
Rape	Rape is the act of forcing penetrative sexual acts, against another's will through violence, force, threat of injury, or other duress, or where the victim is unable to decline, due to the effects of drugs or alcohol.
Delinquency prevention	That which involves any nonjustice program or policy designed to prevent the occurrence of a future delinquent act is referred to as delinquency prevention.
Cohort	A cohort is a group of subjects, most often humans from a given population, defined by experiencing an event (typically birth) in a particular time span.
Strain theory	The proposition that people feel strain when they are exposed to cultural goals that they are unable to obtain because they do not have access to culturally approved means of achieving those goals is strain theory.
Containment theory	A theory suggesting that variation in the crime rates of different social groups is caused by variations in the ability to contain norm-violating behavior in the face of social change and cultural conflict is referred to as containment theory.
Significant other	Significant other is a gender-blind, politically correct term to refer to a person's partner in an intimate relationship without disclosing or presuming anything about his or her marital status or sexual orientation.
Social forces	Social forces are the typical basic drives, or motives, which lead to the fundamental types of association and group relationship.
Folkways	Folkways are the patterns of conventional behavior in a society, norms that apply to everyday matters. They are the conventions and habits learned from childhood.
Mores	Mores are strongly held norms or customs. These derive from the established practices of a society rather than its written laws.
Coping	Efforts to control, reduce, or learn to tolerate the threats that lead to stress is referred to as coping.
Bonding	In the social sciences, the concept of bonding refers to the formation of interpersonal

Go to **Cram101.com** for the Practice Tests for this Chapter.

relationships. Development of emotional attachment between the mother and newborn immediately after birth is considered bonding.

Juvenile delinquency	Juvenile delinquency refers to antisocial or criminal acts performed by minors. It is an important social issue because juveniles are capable of committing serious crimes, but most legal systems prescribe specific procedures and punishments for dealing with such crimes.
Attitude	Attitude refers to an enduring mental representation of a person, place, or thing that evokes an emotional response and related behavior.
Conflict criminology	Largely based on the writings of Karl Marx, conflict criminology claims that crime is inevitable in capitalist societies, as invariably certain groups will become marginalized and unequal. In seeking equality, members of these groups may often turn to crime in order to gain the material wealth that apparently brings equality in capitalist economic states.
Critical criminology	Critical criminology rests upon the fundamental assertion that definitions of what constitute crimes are socially and historically contingent, that is, what constitutes a crime varies in different social situations and different periods of history.
Marxist criminology	Marxist criminology is one of the schools of criminology. It parallels the work of the functionalist school which focuses on what produces stability and continuity in society but, unlike the functionalists, it adopts a predefined political philosophy.
Vested interest	An expectation of private gain that often underlies the expressed interest in a public issue is a vested interest.
Social work	Social work is a helping profession focused on social change, problem solving in human relationships and the empowerment and liberation of people to enhance well-being.
Social behavior	Social behavior is behavior directed towards, or taking place between, members of the same species.
Conglomerate	A collection of companies in different industries that are owned by a single corporation is referred to as a conglomerate.
Sociobiology	Sociobiology is a synthesis of scientific disciplines that attempts to explain behavior in all species by considering the evolutionary advantages of social behaviors. It is often considered a branch of biology and sociology, and it also draws from ethology, evolution, zoology, archeology, population genetics, and other disciplines.
Juvenile justice system	The segment of the justice system including law enforcement officers, the courts, and correctional agencies, designed to treat youthful offenders is referred to as the juvenile justice system.
Restitution	The law of restitution is the law of gains-based recovery. When a court orders restitution it orders the defendant to give up his gains to the claimant.
Addiction	A pattern of behavior characterized by an overwhelming involvement with using a drug and securing its supply is defined as an addiction.
Educational attainment	Educational attainment is a term commonly used by statisticans to refer to the highest degree of education an individual has completed.
Social skills training	Social skills training refers to a behavior therapy designed to improve interpersonal skills that emphasizes shaping, modeling, and behavioral rehearsal.
Social skill	A social skill is a skill used to interact and communicate with others to assist status in the social structure and other motivations. Social rules and social relations are created, communicated, and changed in verbal and nonverbal ways creating social complexity useful in identifying outsiders and intelligent breeding partners.

Go to **Cram101.com** for the Practice Tests for this Chapter.

Moral development	Moral development refers to development regarding rules and conventions about what people should do in their interactions with other people.
Sector	Sector refers to parts of the economy as judged by the economic activity that they constitute. For example agriculture, forestry, fishing and mining constitute the primary sector.
Public policy	Public policy is a course of action or inaction chosen by public authorities to address a problem. Public policy is expressed in the body of laws, regulations, decisions and actions of government.

90

Go to **Cram101.com** for the Practice Tests for this Chapter.

Aggravated Assault	Aggravated assault refers to an unlawful attack by one person upon another for the purpose of inflicting severe or aggravated bodily injury.
Substance abuse	Substance abuse refers to the overindulgence in and dependence on a psychoactive leading to effects that are detrimental to the individual's physical health or mental health, or the welfare of others.
Robbery	The unlawful taking of, or the attempt to take something of value from another person or persons by using violence or the threat of violence, is referred to as a robbery.
Society	A society is a grouping of individuals, which is characterized by common interest and may have distinctive culture and institutions.
Crime	Crime refers to any action that violates criminal laws established by political authority. A crime in a nontechnical sense is an act that violates a very important political or moral command.
Rape	Rape is the act of forcing penetrative sexual acts, against another's will through violence, force, threat of injury, or other duress, or where the victim is unable to decline, due to the effects of drugs or alcohol.
Mental hospital	A medical institution specializing in providing inpatient care for psychological disorders is a psychiatric hospital or mental hospital.
Sex offender	A sex offender is a person who has been criminally charged and convicted of, or has pled guilty to, a sex crime. As a label of identity it is used in criminal psychology.
Probation	Nonpunitive, legal disposition of juveniles emphasizing community treatment in which the juvenile is closely supervized by an officer of the court and must adhere to a strict set of rules to avoid incarceration is probation.
Community	Community refers to a group of people who share a common sense of identity and interact with one another on a sustained basis.
Community service	Community service refers to service that a person performs for the benefit of his or her local community. People become involved in community service for a range of reasons, for some, it is an altruistic act, for others it is a punishment.
Addiction	A pattern of behavior characterized by an overwhelming involvement with using a drug and securing its supply is defined as an addiction.
Narcotic	A narcotic is an addictive drug, derived from opium, that reduces pain, induces sleep and may alter mood or behavior.
Gang	A gang is a group of individuals who share a common identity and, in current usage, engage in illegal activities. Historically the term referred to both criminal groups and ordinary groups of friends.
Disability	A physical or health condition that stigmatizes or causes discrimination, is referred to as a disability.
Aggregate	Aggregate refers to a collection of people who happen to be in the same place at the same time.
Coping	Efforts to control, reduce, or learn to tolerate the threats that lead to stress is referred to as coping.
Criminal justice	Criminal justice refers to the system used by government to maintain social control, enforce laws, and administer justice. Law enforcement (police), courts, and corrections are the primary agencies charged with these responsibilities.
Jurisdiction	Jurisdiction refers to every kind of judicial action; the authority of courts and judicial

	officers to decide cases.
Authority	Authority refers to power that is attached to a position that others perceive as legitimate.
Incest	Incest is sexual activity between close family members. Incest is considered taboo, and forbidden (fully or slightly) in the majority of current cultures.
Arousal	Arousal is a physiological and psychological state involving the activation of the reticular activating system in the brain stem, the autonomic nervous system and the endocrine system, leading to increased heart rate and blood pressure and a condition of alertness and readiness to respond.
Cocaine	Cocaine is a crystalline tropane alkaloid that is obtained from the leaves of the coca plant. It is a stimulant of the central nervous system and an appetite suppressant, creating what has been described as a euphoric sense of happiness and increased energy.
Range	A measure of variability defined as the high score in a distribution minus the low score is referred to as a range.
Attitude	Attitude refers to an enduring mental representation of a person, place, or thing that evokes an emotional response and related behavior.
Deinstitutio-alization	Deinstitutionalization refers to the movement of mental patients out of hospitals and into the community.
Unintended consequence	An unintended consequence comes about when a mechanism that has been installed in the world with the intention of producing one result is used to produce a different (and often conflicting) result.
Date rape	The term, date rape refers to rape or non-consensual sexual activity between people who are already acquainted, or who know each other socially — friends, acquaintances, people on a date, or even people in an existing romantic relationship — where it is alleged that consent for sexual activity was not given, or was given under duress.
Motive	Motive refers to a hypothetical state within an organism that propels the organism toward a goal. In criminal law a motive is the cause that moves people and induce a certain action.
Sex therapy	Sex therapy is the treatment of sexual dysfunction, such as non-consummation, premature ejaculation or erectile dysfunction, low desire, unwanted sexual fetishes, sexual addiction, painful sex or lack of sexual confidence, assist people who are recovering from sexual assault, problems commonly caused by stress, tiredness and other environmental and relationship factors.
Government	A government is a body that has the authority to make and the power to enforce laws within a civil, corporate, religious, academic, or other organization or group.
Neighborhood	A neighborhood is a geographically localized community located within a larger city, town or suburb. Traditionally, a neighborhood is small enough that the neighbors are all able to know each other.
Due process	Basic constitutional principle based on the concept of the primacy of the individual and the complementary concept of limitation on governmental power; safeguards the individual from unfair state procedures in judicial or administrative proceedings; due process rights have been extended to juvenile trials.
Compliance	Conforming behavior that occurs in response to direct social pressure is referred to as compliance.
Heroin	A highly addictive, partly synthetic narcotic derived from morphine is heroin. It mimics endorphins and thus causes a high sense of well-being when entered into the bloodstream (usually through injection).

Addict	A person with an overpowering physical or psychological need to continue taking a particular substance or drug is referred to as an addict.
Organization	In sociology organization is understood as planned, coordinated and purposeful action of human beings to construct or compile a common tangible or intangible product or service.
Wilson	In The Declining Significance of Race: Blacks and Changing American Institutions Wilson argues that the significance of race is waning, and an African-American's class is comparatively more important in determining his or her life chances.
Special language	A language developed by a subgroup in order to set themselves apart from others is a special language.
Violent crime	A violent crime or crime of violence is a crime in which the offender uses or threatens to use violent force upon the victim. The United States Department of Justice Bureau of Justice Statistics (BJS) counts five categories of crime as violent crimes: murder, rape, robbery, aggravated assault, and simple assault.
Depression	In the field of psychiatry, the word depression can also have this meaning of low mood but more specifically refers to a mental illness when it has reached a severity and duration to warrant a diagnosis, whether there is an obvious situational cause or not.
Felony	The term felony is used for very serious crimes, whereas misdemeanors are considered to be less serious offenses. It is a crime punishable by one or more years of imprisonment.
Technology	The application of logic, reason and knowledge to the problems of exploiting raw materials from the environment, is referred to as a technology.
Homelessness	Homelessness refers to the condition and societal category of people who lack housing, or live in transitional housing, or who spend most nights in a supervized public or private facility providing temporary living quarters, or in a public or private place not designed for, or ordinarily used as, a regular sleeping accommodation for human beings.
Aftercare	Transitional assistance to juveniles, equivalent to adult parole, to help youths adjust to community life is the aftercare. Aftercare programs encourage the development of social networks and activities to address emotional needs of recovering alcoholics and substance abusers.
Group therapy	Group therapy is a form of psychotherapy during which one or several therapists treat a small group of clients together as a group. This may be more cost effective than individual therapy, and possibly even more productive.
Recidivism	The probability that those incarcerated and then released are likely to return to prison for the commission of new crimes is referred to as recidivism.
Sexual abuse	Sexual abuse is defined by the forcing of undesired sexual acts by one person to another.
Peer group	A friendship group with common interests and position composed of individuals of similar age is referred to as a peer group.
Social work	Social work is a helping profession focused on social change, problem solving in human relationships and the empowerment and liberation of people to enhance well-being.
Institutiona-ization	The term institutionalization is widely used in social theory to denote the process of making something (for example a concept, a social role, particular values and norms, or modes of behavior) become embedded within an organization, social system, or society as an established custom or norm within that system.
Punishment	Punishment is the practice of imposing something unpleasant on a subject as a response to some unwanted behavior or disobedience that the subject has displayed.

Go to **Cram101.com** for the Practice Tests for this Chapter.

Sexually transmitted disease	Disease transmitted through sexual contact is a sexually transmitted disease.
Sanction	A punishment for nonconformity that reinforces socially approved forms of behavior is a sanction.
Amphetamines	Amphetamines refer to stimulants derived from alpha-methyl-beta-phenyl-ethyl-amine, a colorless liquid consisting of carbon, hydrogen, and nitrogen.
Intake	Intake refers to process during which a juvenile referral is received and a decision is made to file a petition in juvenile court to release the juvenile, to place the juvenile under supervision, or to refer the juvenile elsewhere.
Mean	In statistics, mean has two related meanings: a)the average in ordinary English, which is also called the arithmetic mean (and is distinguished from the geometric mean or harmonic mean). The average is also called sample mean. b)the expected value of a random variable, which is also called the population mean.
Medical model	The application of the medical perspective in explaining and treating troublesome human behavior, is referred to as a medical model.
Electronic monitoring	Electronic monitoring refers to active monitoring systems consist of a radio transmitter worn by the offender that sends a continuous signal to the probation department computer, alerting officials if the offender leaves his or her place of confinement; passive systems employ computer-generated random phone calls that must be responded to in a certain period of time from a particular phone or other device.
Rational choice	Rational choice theory assumes human behavior is guided by instrumental reason. Accordingly, individuals always choose what they believe to be the best means to achieve their given ends. Thus, they are normally regarded as maximizing utility, the "currency" for everything they cherish (for example: money, a long life, moral standards).
Zero tolerance	Zero tolerance is a term used to describe a non-discretionary enforcement policy for the criminal law or informal rules. Under a system of zero tolerance, persons in positions of authority – who might otherwise exercise their discretion in making subjective judgments regarding the severity of a given offense – are instead compelled to act in particular ways and, where relevant, to impose a pre-determined punishment regardless of individual culpability.
Tolerance	Tolerance is a recent political term used within debates in areas of social, cultural and religious context, as an emphatic antithesis to discrimination, as such may advocate persecution. Its usage came about as a more widely acceptable alternative to "acceptance", the usage of which had been widely derided, as certain cases would not be considered by common society as acceptable.
Baseline	Measure of a particular behavior or process taken before the introduction of the independent variable or treatment is referred to as a baseline.
Battery	In many common law jurisdictions, the crime of battery involves an injury or other contact upon the person of another in a manner likely to cause bodily harm.
Detention	Temporary care of a child alleged to be delinquent who requires secure custody in physically restricting facilities pending court disposition or execution of a court order is detention.
Control group	A group of people in an experiment who are not exposed to the experimental stimulus under study are referred to as a control group.
Social support	Social support is the physical and emotional comfort given to us by our family, friends, co-workers and others. It is knowing that we are part of a community of people who love and care

	for us, and value and think well of us.
Empathy	Empathy is commonly defined as one's ability to recognize, perceive and directly experientially feel the emotion of another. As the states of mind, beliefs, and desires of others are intertwined with their emotions, one with empathy for another may often be able to more effectively divine another's modes of thought and mood.
Frequency	In statistics the frequency of an event i is the number n_i of times the event occurred in the experiment or the study.
Social skill	A social skill is a skill used to interact and communicate with others to assist status in the social structure and other motivations. Social rules and social relations are created, communicated, and changed in verbal and nonverbal ways creating social complexity useful in identifying outsiders and intelligent breeding partners.
Reinforcement contingencies	The circumstances or rules that determine whether responses lead to the presentation of reinforcers are referred to as reinforcement contingencies.
Reinforcement	A stimulus that follows a response and increases the frequency of the response is a reinforcement.
Methodology	Methodology is defined as (1) "a body of methods, rules, and postulates employed by a discipline", (2)"a particular procedure or set of procedures", or (3)"the analysis of the principles or procedures of inquiry in a particular field".
Public policy	Public policy is a course of action or inaction chosen by public authorities to address a problem. Public policy is expressed in the body of laws, regulations, decisions and actions of government.

Juvenile court	Court that has original jurisdiction over persons defined by statute as juveniles and alleged to be delinquents, status offenders, or dependents is called juvenile court.
Authority	Authority refers to power that is attached to a position that others perceive as legitimate.
Probation	Nonpunitive, legal disposition of juveniles emphasizing community treatment in which the juvenile is closely supervized by an officer of the court and must adhere to a strict set of rules to avoid incarceration is probation.
Community	Community refers to a group of people who share a common sense of identity and interact with one another on a sustained basis.
Sex offender	A sex offender is a person who has been criminally charged and convicted of, or has pled guilty to, a sex crime. As a label of identity it is used in criminal psychology.
Acquisition	The initial learning of the stimulus response link, which involves a neutral stimulus being associated with a UCS and becoming a conditioned stimulus, is referred to as an acquisition.
Empathy	Empathy is commonly defined as one's ability to recognize, perceive and directly experientially feel the emotion of another. As the states of mind, beliefs, and desires of others are intertwined with their emotions, one with empathy for another may often be able to more effectively divine another's modes of thought and mood.
Jurisdiction	Jurisdiction refers to every kind of judicial action; the authority of courts and judicial officers to decide cases.
Deinstitutio-alization	Deinstitutionalization refers to the movement of mental patients out of hospitals and into the community.
Parens patriae	Parens patriae refers to power of the state to act in behalf of the child and provide care and protection equivalent to that of a parent.
Juvenile justice system	The segment of the justice system including law enforcement officers, the courts, and correctional agencies, designed to treat youthful offenders is referred to as the juvenile justice system.
Intake	Intake refers to process during which a juvenile referral is received and a decision is made to file a petition in juvenile court to release the juvenile, to place the juvenile under supervision, or to refer the juvenile elsewhere.
Juvenile delinquency	Juvenile delinquency refers to antisocial or criminal acts performed by minors. It is an important social issue because juveniles are capable of committing serious crimes, but most legal systems prescribe specific procedures and punishments for dealing with such crimes.
Criminal law	Criminal law (also known as penal law) is the body of statutory and common law that deals with crime and the legal punishment of criminal offenses. There are four theories of criminal justice: punishment, deterrence, incapacitation, and rehabilitation.
Mens rea	The mens rea is the Latin term for "guilty mind" used in the criminal law. In jurisdictions with due process, there must be an actus reus accompanied by some level of mens rea to constitute the crime with which the defendant is charged.
Punishment	Punishment is the practice of imposing something unpleasant on a subject as a response to some unwanted behavior or disobedience that the subject has displayed.
Status offense	A status offense is an action that is a crime only if the perpetrator is a minor. For instance, consumption of alcohol by a minor may be a status offense in jurisdictions where such consumption is permitted, but only by persons over a specified age.
Crime	Crime refers to any action that violates criminal laws established by political authority. A crime in a nontechnical sense is an act that violates a very important political or moral

command.

Liquor law	Liquor law is a term that refers to any legislation dealing with the abolishment, restriction, or regulation of the sale, consumption, and manufacture of alcoholic beverages.
Organization	In sociology organization is understood as planned, coordinated and purposeful action of human beings to construct or compile a common tangible or intangible product or service.
Government	A government is a body that has the authority to make and the power to enforce laws within a civil, corporate, religious, academic, or other organization or group.
Mean	In statistics, mean has two related meanings: a)the average in ordinary English, which is also called the arithmetic mean (and is distinguished from the geometric mean or harmonic mean). The average is also called sample mean. b)the expected value of a random variable, which is also called the population mean.
Society	A society is a grouping of individuals, which is characterized by common interest and may have distinctive culture and institutions.
Innovations	A concept created by Robert Merton to describe the way norms assist in achieving goals are referred to as innovations.
Parsons	Parsons was an advocate of "grand theory," an attempt to integrate all the social sciences into an overarching theoretical framework. His early work — The Structure of Social Action —reviewed the output of his great predecessors, especially Max Weber, Vilfredo Pareto, and Émile Durkheim, and attempted to derive from them a single "action theory" based on the assumptions that human action is voluntary, intentional, and symbolic.
Division of labor	Division of labor is the specialisation of cooperative labor in specific, circumscribed tasks and roles, intended to increase efficiency of output.
Migration	The movement of people from one country or region to another in order to settle permanently, is referred to as a migration.
Reform school	A reform school in the United States was a term used to define, often somewhat euphemistically, what was often essentially a penal institution for boys, generally teenagers.
Public defender	In the United States, a public defender is a lawyer whose duty is to provide legal counsel and representation to indigent defendants in criminal cases who are unable to pay for legal assistance.
Criminal justice	Criminal justice refers to the system used by government to maintain social control, enforce laws, and administer justice. Law enforcement (police), courts, and corrections are the primary agencies charged with these responsibilities.
Statistics	Statistics is a mathematical science pertaining to the collection, analysis, interpretation, and presentation of data. It is applicable to a wide variety of academic disciplines, from the physical and social sciences to the humanities; it is also used and misused for making informed decisions in all areas of business and government.
Reinforcement	A stimulus that follows a response and increases the frequency of the response is a reinforcement.
Range	A measure of variability defined as the high score in a distribution minus the low score is referred to as a range.
Community service	Community service refers to service that a person performs for the benefit of his or her local community. People become involved in community service for a range of reasons, for some, it is an altruistic act, for others it is a punishment.

Restitution	The law of restitution is the law of gains-based recovery. When a court orders restitution it orders the defendant to give up his gains to the claimant.
Sanction	A punishment for nonconformity that reinforces socially approved forms of behavior is a sanction.
Social problem	A social condition that is perceived as having harmful effects is a social problem. Opinions about whether a condition is a social problem vary among groups and depend upon how and by whom the condition is defined and perceived in society.
Life chances	Life chances are the opportunities each individual has to improve their quality of life. The concept was introduced by German sociologist Max Weber. It is a probabilistic concept, describing how likely it is, given certain factors, that an individual's life will turn out a certain way.
Detention	Temporary care of a child alleged to be delinquent who requires secure custody in physically restricting facilities pending court disposition or execution of a court order is detention.
Due process	Basic constitutional principle based on the concept of the primacy of the individual and the complementary concept of limitation on governmental power; safeguards the individual from unfair state procedures in judicial or administrative proceedings; due process rights have been extended to juvenile trials.
Detention hearing	Detention hearing refers to a hearing by a judicial officer of a juvenile court to determine whether a juvenile is to be detained or released while juvenile proceedings are pending in the case.
Waiver	A waiver is the voluntary relinquishment or surrender of some known right or privilege. While a waiver is often in writing, sometimes a person's actions can act as a waiver. An example of a written waiver is a disclaimer, which becomes a waiver when accepted. Other names for waivers are exculpatory clauses, releases, or hold harmless clauses.
Aggravated Assault	Aggravated assault refers to an unlawful attack by one person upon another for the purpose of inflicting severe or aggravated bodily injury.
Robbery	The unlawful taking of, or the attempt to take something of value from another person or persons by using violence or the threat of violence, is referred to as a robbery.
Rape	Rape is the act of forcing penetrative sexual acts, against another's will through violence, force, threat of injury, or other duress, or where the victim is unable to decline, due to the effects of drugs or alcohol.
Murder	Murder is the unlawful, premeditated killing of a human being by another. The penalty for murder is usually either life imprisonment, or in jurisdictions with capital punishment, the death penalty.
Capital punishment	Use of the death penalty to punish offenders is called capital punishment.
Judicial waiver	Judicial waiver is when a juvenile court waives its jurisdiction over a juvenile and transfers the case to adult criminal court.
Felony	The term felony is used for very serious crimes, whereas misdemeanors are considered to be less serious offenses. It is a crime punishable by one or more years of imprisonment.
Violent crime	A violent crime or crime of violence is a crime in which the offender uses or threatens to use violent force upon the victim. The United States Department of Justice Bureau of Justice Statistics (BJS) counts five categories of crime as violent crimes: murder, rape, robbery, aggravated assault, and simple assault.
Probable cause	Reasonable ground to believe the existence of facts that an offense was committed and that

Go to **Cram101.com** for the Practice Tests for this Chapter.

the accused committed that offense is called probable cause.

Attitude	Attitude refers to an enduring mental representation of a person, place, or thing that evokes an emotional response and related behavior.
Concurrent jurisdiction	Concurrent jurisdiction exists where two or more courts from different systems simultaneously have jurisdiction over a specific case.
Excluded offenses	Excluded offenses refers to offenses, some minor and others very serious, that are automatically excluded from juvenile court and are placed under the jurisdiction of an adult criminal court.
Transfer hearing	Preadjudicatory hearing in juvenile court for the purpose of determining whether juvenile court should be retained over a juvenile or waived and the juvenile transferred to adult court for prosecution is referred to as transfer hearing.
Fingerprint	A fingerprint is an impression of the friction ridges of all or any part of the finger. They may be deposited in natural secretions from the eccrine glands present in friction ridge skin or they may be made by ink or other contaminants transferred from the peaks of friction skin ridges to a relatively smooth surface such as a fingerprint card.
Larceny	Larceny is the trespassory taking and asportation of the (tangible) personal property of another with the intent to deprive him or her of it permanently.
Double jeopardy	Double jeopardy (also called "autrefois acquit" meaning "already acquitted") is a procedural defense (and, in many countries such as the United States, Canada, and India, a constitutional right) that forbids a defendant from being tried a second time for a crime, after having already been tried for the same crime.
Preventive detention	Keeping the accused in custody prior to trial because the accused is suspected of being a danger to the community is called preventive detention.
Group home	A Group home is a structure designed or converted to serve as a non-secure home for persons who share a common characteristic. In the United States, the term most often refers to homes designed for those in need of social assistance, and who are usually deemed incapable of living alone or without proper supervision.
Delinquency prevention	That which involves any nonjustice program or policy designed to prevent the occurrence of a future delinquent act is referred to as delinquency prevention.
Psychotherapy	Psychotherapy refers to a systematic interaction between a therapist and a client that brings psychological principles to bear on influencing the client's thoughts, feelings, or behavior to help that client overcome abnormal behavior or adjust to problems in living.
Recidivism	The probability that those incarcerated and then released are likely to return to prison for the commission of new crimes is referred to as recidivism.
Gender	Gender refers to socially defined behavior regarded as appropriate for the members of each
Family group homes	Family group homes refers to a combination of foster care and a group home in which a juvenile is placed in a private group home run by a single family rather than by professional staff.
Peer group	A friendship group with common interests and position composed of individuals of similar age is referred to as a peer group.
Alcoholism	Alcoholism refers to a disorder that involves long-term, repeated, uncontrolled, compulsive, and excessive use of alcoholic beverages and that impairs the drinker's health, work and social relationships.
Victim impact	A victim impact statement is a written or verbal statement made as part of the judicial legal

statement	process, which allows a victim of crime the opportunity to speak during the sentencing of their attacker or at subsequent parole hearings.
Group therapy	Group therapy is a form of psychotherapy during which one or several therapists treat a small group of clients together as a group. This may be more cost effective than individual therapy, and possibly even more productive.
Burglary	Burglary – also called breaking and entering or house breaking – is a crime related to theft. It typically involves someone breaking into a house with an intent to commit a crime.
Aftercare	Transitional assistance to juveniles, equivalent to adult parole, to help youths adjust to community life is the aftercare. Aftercare programs encourage the development of social networks and activities to address emotional needs of recovering alcoholics and substance abusers.
House arrest	House arrest refers to an offender is required to stay at home during specific periods of time; monitoring is done by random phone calls and visits or by electronic devices.
Substance abuse	Substance abuse refers to the overindulgence in and dependence on a psychoactive leading to effects that are detrimental to the individual's physical health or mental health, or the welfare of others.
Aggregate	Aggregate refers to a collection of people who happen to be in the same place at the same time.
Control group	A group of people in an experiment who are not exposed to the experimental stimulus under study are referred to as a control group.
Electronic monitoring	Electronic monitoring refers to active monitoring systems consist of a radio transmitter worn by the offender that sends a continuous signal to the probation department computer, alerting officials if the offender leaves his or her place of confinement; passive systems employ computer-generated random phone calls that must be responded to in a certain period of time from a particular phone or other device.
Peer pressure	Peer pressure comprises a set of group dynamics whereby a group of people in which one feels comfortable may override the personal habits, individual moral inhibitions or idiosyncratic desires to impose a group norm of attitudes or behaviors.
Sexual assault	Sexual assault is any undesired physical contact of a sexual nature perpetrated against another person. While associated with rape, sexual assault is much broader and the specifics may vary according to social, political or legal definition.
Adaptation	Adaptation refers to the ability of a sociocultural system to change with the demands of a changing physical or social environment.
Endemic	In epidemiology, an infection is said to be endemic in a population when that infection is maintained in the population without the need for external inputs.
Typology	Typology refers to the classification of observations in terms of their attributes on two or more variables. The classification of newspapers as liberal-urban, liberal-rural, conservative-urban, or conservative-rural would be an example of a typology.
Case law	Case law is the body of judge-made law and legal decisions that interprets prior case law, statutes and other legal authority -- including doctrinal writings by legal scholars such as the Corpus Juris Secundum, Halsbury's Laws of England or the doctrinal writings found in the Recueil Dalloz and law commissions such as the American Law Institute.
Battery	In many common law jurisdictions, the crime of battery involves an injury or other contact upon the person of another in a manner likely to cause bodily harm.
Gang	A gang is a group of individuals who share a common identity and, in current usage, engage in

	illegal activities. Historically the term referred to both criminal groups and ordinary groups of friends.
Compliance	Conforming behavior that occurs in response to direct social pressure is referred to as compliance.
Coping	Efforts to control, reduce, or learn to tolerate the threats that lead to stress is referred to as coping.
Restorative justice	Restorative justice is commonly known as a theory of criminal justice that focuses on crime as an act against another individual or community rather than the state. The victim plays a major role in the process and may receive some type of restitution from the offender.

112

Go to **Cram101.com** for the Practice Tests for this Chapter.

Recidivism	The probability that those incarcerated and then released are likely to return to prison for the commission of new crimes is referred to as recidivism.
Juvenile delinquency	Juvenile delinquency refers to antisocial or criminal acts performed by minors. It is an important social issue because juveniles are capable of committing serious crimes, but most legal systems prescribe specific procedures and punishments for dealing with such crimes.
Institutiona- ization	The term institutionalization is widely used in social theory to denote the process of making something (for example a concept, a social role, particular values and norms, or modes of behavior) become embedded within an organization, social system, or society as an established custom or norm within that system.
Residential programs	Placement of a juvenile offender in a residential, nonsecure facility such as a group home, foster home, family group home, or rural home where the juvenile can be closely monitored and develop close relationships with staff members is referred to as residential programs.
Substance abuse	Substance abuse refers to the overindulgence in and dependence on a psychoactive leading to effects that are detrimental to the individual's physical health or mental health, or the welfare of others.
Probation	Nonpunitive, legal disposition of juveniles emphasizing community treatment in which the juvenile is closely supervized by an officer of the court and must adhere to a strict set of rules to avoid incarceration is probation.
Sanction	A punishment for nonconformity that reinforces socially approved forms of behavior is a sanction.
Electronic monitoring	Electronic monitoring refers to active monitoring systems consist of a radio transmitter worn by the offender that sends a continuous signal to the probation department computer, alerting officials if the offender leaves his or her place of confinement; passive systems employ computer-generated random phone calls that must be responded to in a certain period of time from a particular phone or other device.
House arrest	House arrest refers to an offender is required to stay at home during specific periods of time; monitoring is done by random phone calls and visits or by electronic devices.
Variable	A characteristic that varies in value or magnitude along which an object, individual or group may be categorized, such as income or age, is referred to as a variable.
Gender	Gender refers to socially defined behavior regarded as appropriate for the members of each
Control group	A group of people in an experiment who are not exposed to the experimental stimulus under study are referred to as a control group.
Statistics	Statistics is a mathematical science pertaining to the collection, analysis, interpretation, and presentation of data. It is applicable to a wide variety of academic disciplines, from the physical and social sciences to the humanities; it is also used and misused for making informed decisions in all areas of business and government.
Felony	The term felony is used for very serious crimes, whereas misdemeanors are considered to be less serious offenses. It is a crime punishable by one or more years of imprisonment.
Restitution	The law of restitution is the law of gains-based recovery. When a court orders restitution it orders the defendant to give up his gains to the claimant.
Organization	In sociology organization is understood as planned, coordinated and purposeful action of human beings to construct or compile a common tangible or intangible product or service.
Response rate	Response rate refers to the number of people participating in a survey divided by the number selected in the sample, in the form of a percentage. This is also called the completion rate or, in self-administered surveys, or the return rate.

Go to **Cram101.com** for the Practice Tests for this Chapter.

Community	Community refers to a group of people who share a common sense of identity and interact with one another on a sustained basis.
Compliance	Conforming behavior that occurs in response to direct social pressure is referred to as compliance.
Crime	Crime refers to any action that violates criminal laws established by political authority. A crime in a nontechnical sense is an act that violates a very important political or moral command.
Sex offender	A sex offender is a person who has been criminally charged and convicted of, or has pled guilty to, a sex crime. As a label of identity it is used in criminal psychology.
Mean	In statistics, mean has two related meanings: a)the average in ordinary English, which is also called the arithmetic mean (and is distinguished from the geometric mean or harmonic mean). The average is also called sample mean. b)the expected value of a random variable, which is also called the population mean.
Criminal justice	Criminal justice refers to the system used by government to maintain social control, enforce laws, and administer justice. Law enforcement (police), courts, and corrections are the primary agencies charged with these responsibilities.
Aggregate	Aggregate refers to a collection of people who happen to be in the same place at the same time.
Spousal abuse	Spousal abuse is a specific form of domestic violence where physical or sexual abuse is perpetuated by one spouse upon another.
Group therapy	Group therapy is a form of psychotherapy during which one or several therapists treat a small group of clients together as a group. This may be more cost effective than individual therapy, and possibly even more productive.
Alcoholism	Alcoholism refers to a disorder that involves long-term, repeated, uncontrolled, compulsive, and excessive use of alcoholic beverages and that impairs the drinker's health, work and social relationships.
Jurisdiction	Jurisdiction refers to every kind of judicial action; the authority of courts and judicial officers to decide cases.
Consensus	Agreement on basic social values by the members of a group or society is referred to as a consensus.
Criminologist	A criminologist is often defined as someone who studies the aetiology of crime, criminal behavior, types of crime, and social, cultural and media reactions to crime.
Frequency	In statistics the frequency of an event i is the number n_i of times the event occurred in the experiment or the study.
Validity	The degree to which a measurement instrument measures what it is intended to measure is referred to as validity.
Government	A government is a body that has the authority to make and the power to enforce laws within a civil, corporate, religious, academic, or other organization or group.
Authority	Authority refers to power that is attached to a position that others perceive as legitimate.
Neighborhood	A neighborhood is a geographically localized community located within a larger city, town or suburb. Traditionally, a neighborhood is small enough that the neighbors are all able to know each other.
Probable cause	Reasonable ground to believe the existence of facts that an offense was committed and that the accused committed that offense is called probable cause.

Go to Cram101.com for the Practice Tests for this Chapter.

Burglary	Burglary – also called breaking and entering or house breaking – is a crime related to theft. It typically involves someone breaking into a house with an intent to commit a crime.
Larceny	Larceny is the trespassory taking and asportation of the (tangible) personal property of another with the intent to deprive him or her of it permanently.
Community service	Community service refers to service that a person performs for the benefit of his or her local community. People become involved in community service for a range of reasons, for some, it is an altruistic act, for others it is a punishment.
Vested interest	An expectation of private gain that often underlies the expressed interest in a public issue is a vested interest.
Detention	Temporary care of a child alleged to be delinquent who requires secure custody in physically restricting facilities pending court disposition or execution of a court order is detention.
Range	A measure of variability defined as the high score in a distribution minus the low score is referred to as a range.
Public policy	Public policy is a course of action or inaction chosen by public authorities to address a problem. Public policy is expressed in the body of laws, regulations, decisions and actions of government.
Punishment	Punishment is the practice of imposing something unpleasant on a subject as a response to some unwanted behavior or disobedience that the subject has displayed.
Insanity	Insanity refers to a legal status indicating that a person cannot be held responsible for his or her actions because of mental illness.
Robbery	The unlawful taking of, or the attempt to take something of value from another person or persons by using violence or the threat of violence, is referred to as a robbery.
Society	A society is a grouping of individuals, which is characterized by common interest and may have distinctive culture and institutions.
Wilson	In The Declining Significance of Race: Blacks and Changing American Institutions Wilson argues that the significance of race is waning, and an African-American's class is comparatively more important in determining his or her life chances.

CPSIA information can be obtained at www.ICGtesting.com
Printed in the USA
BVOW06s0219020215

385970BV00002B/29/P